Understanding China

PRAEGER LIBRARY OF CHINESE AFFAIRS

General Editor: Donald W. Klein, Columbia University

China is one of the world's oldest civilizations and one of the least known or understood. Its rich history has much to contribute to our understanding of man; its experiences in modernization are relevant to other developing nations; its crucial role in Asian and world politics makes imperative a fuller comprehension of the Chinese past and present.

The volumes in this multidisciplinary series will explore central issues of China's political, social, and economic structure, its foreign relations, its philosophy and thought, and its history, civilization, and culture. The contributors to the series represent a wide variety of approaches and attitudes, and all are specialists in their respective fields. Included in the series are the following works:

Ralph C. Croizier, ed., *China's Cultural Legacy and Communism* (1970)

Alexander Eckstein, ed., *China Trade Prospects and U.S. Policy* (1971)

Donald G. Gillin, *History of the Chinese Civil War, 1945–50* (1972)*

James P. Harrison, *A History of the Chinese Communist Party* (1972)*

Li Jui, *Comrade Mao Tse-tung's Early Revolutionary Activities*, trans. by Anthony W. Sariti, with an introduction by Stuart R. Schram (1972)*

John M. H. Lindbeck, *Understanding China: An Assessment of American Scholarly Resources* (1971)

Michel Oksenberg and Frederick C. Teiwes, eds., *The Chinese Communist Bureaucracy at Work* (1972)*

Lucian W. Pye, *Warlord Politics: Conflict and Coalition in the Modernization of Republican China* (1971)

Theodore Shabad, *China's Changing Map: National and Regional Development, 1949–71*, rev. ed. (1972)

William W. Whitson, with Chen-hsia Huang, *The Chinese Communist High Command: A History of Military Politics, 1927–70* (1972)*

* *Title and publication date are not yet final.*

Understanding China

An Assessment of American Scholarly Resources

JOHN M. H. LINDBECK

With a Foreword by A. Doak Barnett

A Report to the Ford Foundation

PRAEGER PUBLISHERS

New York • Washington • London

PRAEGER PUBLISHERS
111 Fourth Avenue, New York, N.Y. 10003, U.S.A.
5, Cromwell Place, London SW7 2JL, England

Published in the United States of America in 1971
by Praeger Publishers, Inc.

© 1971 by Praeger Publishers, Inc.

Library of Congress Catalog Card Number: 76-175626

Printed in the United States of America

Contents

Tables

Foreword

This survey and analysis of China studies was written in 1970 by Professor John M. H. Lindbeck for the Ford Foundation. It focuses on the growth of modern and contemporary China studies in the United States during the 1960's, a period which Professor Lindbeck quite rightly calls a "developmental decade."

The report highlights both accomplishments and problems and contains a great deal of significant information including data on the organization of the field, its growth in terms of numbers of active scholars and students, the expansion of institutional centers concerned with China studies, the large increase in financial support of the field, and so on. The study also discusses a variety of problems, both old and new. In the conclusions, the author presents his views on needs and priorities for the future—first of all, what is needed to sustain and preserve the resources built up during the past decade, and, beyond that, what some of the requirements are for continued development of the field during the decade ahead.

The principal stimulus, in intellectual and substantive terms, for the rapid development of modern and contemporary China studies in the United States during the 1960's came, quite naturally, from the scholarly community itself. The Ford Foundation, in response to this stimulus, played a major role in supporting and financing the developmental process. Between 1959 and 1970, the Foundation gave grants to the China field totaling more than $23 million to assist university centers and programs, provide needed fellowships, support research, and assist a variety of national and international organizational activities and projects.

In addition to the Foundation's investment in the China field during this period, the U.S. Government provided support amounting to about $15 million, mainly for fellowships, and American universities themselves invested a comparable amount. In view of its considerable assistance to China studies, the Foundation decided in 1969 to request a respected scholar in the field to make an independent evaluation not only of what had resulted from its investment in the field but also of the broader accomplishments and problems of this developmental process.

The choice of Professor Lindbeck to make the study was most fortunate. He was uniquely qualified for the assignment. As a scholar, he was completely committed to the task of developing knowledge and understanding of China, both in the United States and abroad; he was also fully trusted by his colleagues in the China field and admired both for his broad vision and for his intellectual integrity and objectivity.

Born in China, Professor Lindbeck was thoroughly trained as a China scholar. His doctorate was obtained at Yale, and he pursued additional graduate work at Harvard. After teaching at Yale, he spent a number of years in government service and then returned to academic pursuits in 1958.

From 1958 until his death in 1971, Professor Lindbeck was at the forefront of the process of planning, stimulating, promoting, and organizing the developmental process in the field of modern and contemporary China studies. He himself, in short, played a leading role in the "developmental decade." Yet, as a great many people—including his closest colleagues—will testify, he always was able to examine the field with detachment and objectivity.

Professor Lindbeck played a key role in fostering scholarly work on modern and contemporary China at two of the principal university centers of China studies in the United States. From 1959 to 1967, he was associate director of the East Asian Research Center at Harvard, and from 1967 on he was director of the East Asian Institute at Columbia.

Equally important, he was an organizer and leader in many national and international programs and organizations that played a crucial role in developing the field. These included: the Joint Committee on Contemporary China (of the American Council of Learned Societies [ACLS] and the Social Science Research Council [SSRC]), which he chaired for six years, from 1964 to 1970; the Committee on Scholarly Communication with the People's Republic of China (sponsored by the National Academy of Sciences as well as the ACLS and SSRC), which he chaired from 1968 on; the international Liaison Committee on the Study of Contemporary China; the National Committee on United States–China Relations; and many others.

When he undertook to make this study, Professor Lindbeck was able to draw extensively upon his own accumulated knowledge and experience. In addition, he spent the better part of a year talking to hundreds of scholars and students in the United States and visiting universities and research centers throughout Asia and Europe. In the latter part of 1970, he started to write up the results of his work. As the reader of this volume will see, he completed his assessment of this country's scholarly resources for understanding China. He was not, however, able to carry out in full the report he had originally planned. Professor

Lindbeck died suddenly in January, 1971—just a few months before China's tentative new overtures to the West.

Professor Lindbeck's original plan had called for the report to cover the development of both scholarly studies and public-affairs resources for understanding China in other countries as well as the United States. At the time of his death, however, he had only begun to put on paper his data and ideas concerning scholarly work abroad, and on programs to foster broad public understanding in the United States. Hence, these topics had to be excluded from this volume. (It is especially tragic that he was not able to complete the portion of the study dealing with China studies in areas other than the United States, because he probably knew more about this subject than any other American scholar.)

This report as now published focuses on the development of scholarly resources in the United States for the study of modern and contemporary China. It contains only material written by Professor Lindbeck, and completed before his death, plus some of the appendixes he had prepared.

Professor Lindbeck starts by analyzing the variety of motivations and patterns shaping China studies. Thereafter, the bulk of the report discusses the development of the field during the 1960's, surveying in considerable detail the growth of university programs and centers, the organization of the field at the national level, and many other topics, including fellowship support for students, support for research, and the development of overseas training facilities. Throughout the study, the author highlights developmental problems, both in the past and in the future.

In the final sections of the report, Professor Lindbeck outlines a number of conclusions and recommendations. Some of these are stated only briefly, and there is little doubt that if he had lived he would have elaborated upon many of them at greater length. Nevertheless, even without further elaboration, they are of great value. The report, as it now stands, is an extremely significant contribution to the field of China studies, and its publication is a tribute, also, to Professor Lindbeck's life and work.

If Professor Lindbeck had lived, he would almost certainly have been the first to insist that the report in its present form should be regarded as only a first step toward an evaluation of past accomplishments, problems, and needs for the future. There is still a need, for example, for a thorough analysis—qualitative as well as quantitative—of the research output in this field to date, comparable to the assessments that have been attempted in recent years in the Soviet studies and Japan studies fields.

The most important thing about the report, however, is not that Professor Lindbeck was unable to do all that he had hoped to do, but that the report is clearly one of the most valuable studies of its kind to have been done in the China field, for it is full of invaluable data, analysis, and insights.

Looking to the future, Professor Lindbeck stresses that the 1970's will present a variety of challenges and problems quite different from those of the 1960's. The major challenge will be to preserve and improve upon what has been built up during the past decade, to ensure that the newly trained generation of scholars and the newly built institutional structures can be fully and effectively utilized, to make a major effort to raise the level of scholarship in qualitative terms, and to foster new programs to broaden public understanding of China.

As Professor Lindbeck suggests, one cannot expect all of these aims to be achieved automatically; in fact, one cannot by any means assume that they will necessarily be achieved at all. Further progress in developing the field and widening its impact in the 1970's will require, during the decade ahead, the kind of dedication, commitment, and tireless effort that Professor Lindbeck and others contributed to the field in the 1960's.

A. DOAK BARNETT

The Brookings Institution
Washington, D.C.
June, 1971

Understanding China

I. Chinese Studies: Motivations and Patterns

In the world today, the People's Republic of China is more isolated than any other major nation. It is an inescapable and constant challenge to world understanding. In view of its size and location, the historic strength and powerful influence of its traditional culture, and the fears, uncertainties, and attractions it has engendered during the past two decades, China's isolation is perplexing and anomalous. More than half of the nations of the world, including the United States, have yet to find a basis acceptable to themselves and to the Chinese for observing the minimum civilities of diplomatic and international intercourse.

Millions of aerial and other photographs make its terrain familiar in detail to government specialists of other countries. A steady flood of words directed by the Chinese at domestic and foreign audiences portrays its official policies and views to all who read or listen. What goes on, however, beneath the surface is obscure. How China's long past relates to its present revolution is equally unclear.

The reasons for learning about China differ from country to country, but certain characteristic national patterns of motivation emerge. These diverse purposes help to explain the nature of the programs for studying and observing China in different countries and institutions.

1/ First, within the Chinese cultural zone, China is part of the classical heritage of millions of people. This zone includes such countries and communities as Singapore, Taiwan, Hong Kong, Korea, Japan, Vietnam, and the Chinese minorities in Southeast Asia, the Americas, and elsewhere. These people have a natural desire to return to Chinese sources to sustain a particular culture and its traditions

2/ Second, outside the Chinese cultural sphere, the Western study of China began in the nineteenth century primarily to meet missionary and business needs. After 1840, the British Government began a formal program of training Chinese specialists at the University of London; by the end of the century, the United States had established a program for training diplomats in Chinese. These interests later broadened to encompass the scholarly traditions associated with "liberal" values and education—the intellectual impulse to comprehend all varieties of human experience and to reach a balanced picture of the world. This liberal view has continued to play and important part in sustaining and shaping Chinese studies in Europe and the United States.

3/ Third, in the post–World War II transformation of the world as new national states rose and the old imperial order collapsed, the search for new strategies of development, revolution, or warfare has focused attention on China from groups with widely divergent interests.

4. Fourth, commercial and economic interests in a few countries have mobilized some support for programs of training and research.

5. Fifth, varied political concerns have made China the subject of steady scrutiny and study. Some wish to develop more satisfactory political relations with China, others to

involve China in international political processes. Still others wish to frustrate its ambitions. Some, on the other hand, want to gain China's support against domestic or foreign enemies and to use it to promote their own domestic or international political purposes.

Sixth, during the past two decades, fear of China's growing military power, actual and potential, has led many governments to establish training and research programs so as to better monitor Chinese activities and development. Thus, security considerations have directly and indirectly inspired a wide range of Chinese studies. Governmental programs, far exceeding the total range of scholarly and other unofficial efforts to understand China, are mostly hidden from public view in all countries. In some countries, they are closely related to scholarly programs, in others, almost entirely separate.

One conclusion of a survey of Chinese studies around the world is that the scholarly study of China has developed only in countries with several motives for seeking to understand China and with agreement on its relevance among individuals, groups, and official agencies that control the substantial resources needed for training and research. Apart from mainland China and Taiwan, thus far only twelve of more than 120 political entities around the world have developed self-sustaining programs of Chinese studies. About thirteen more include the study of China in one or more institutions of higher education.* One concern usu-

---

* The following twelve countries have sufficient resources and scholars to train their own specialists at an advanced level, that is, award a doctorate, in more than one area in the China field: Australia, Canada, Czechoslovakia, Denmark, France, Germany, Japan, the Netherlands, Sweden, the United Kingdom, the United States, and the Soviet Union.

Thirteen countries with limited programs of professional quality are: Austria, Belgium, Hong Kong, Hungary, India, Israel, Italy, Malaysia, Norway, Philippines, Poland, Singapore, East Germany. Seven others have initiated programs that may be developed: Chile, Finland, Indonesia, Mexico, South Korea, Thailand, New Zealand.

ally seems dominant among the several motives for Chinese studies in a particular country, although the center of interest may shift, depending on such factors as the character and perceptions of the national leadership, the influence of important sectors of the population, the nature of a country's relationship with China, and the place of Chinese studies in a nation's educational system and scholarly traditions.

In Asia, Africa, Latin America, the Middle East

Within the Chinese cultural sphere, knowledge of the traditional civilization of China is an accepted part of historical, literary, and cultural studies, necessary for national self-understanding. However, because of the low priority given to humanistic studies in the postwar period, there is very little advanced training and research on premodern China, with some exceptions in Japan. Furthermore, the scholarly study of contemporary China is not encouraged, is usually restricted, and often forbidden. Because political and military relations with China of all the non-Communist states within this region are uneasy or hostile, governments seek to discourage or prevent the circulation of information and views about China that are considered politically undesirable.

Thus, Taiwan, Hong Kong, Singapore, Korea, and Japan have fairly substantial resources for the scholarly study of pre-1949 China, but scholarship on contemporary China is either restricted or given little or no encouragement. In Hong Kong, it is essentially limited to private groups. Taiwan bars the circulation of all Communist Chinese publications, as do Singapore and South Korea. In Japan, students and scholars are reported to be far more interested in the United States and Europe; programs on China are modest; scholarly research on contemporary China primarily depends on government contracts and institutes, and on the research departments of newspapers and political parties, which support them for their own professional purposes. At the same time, government agencies in some of these countries, such as Taiwan and Japan, have developed fairly substantial intelligence and research capabilities, with the usual policy orientations, for studying current Chinese affairs.

In other parts of Asia, the political and security interests that tend to predominate have not provided the necessary stimulus for the development of scholarly resources for Chinese studies. In India, for example, the military threat of China led the government to train a few able analysts to meet needs in foreign affairs, intelligence, and defense. However, the result has not been to mobilize requisite resources for substantial academic and public-affairs programs relating to China. The Indian intellectual community apparently includes few who believe that Chinese experience, past or present, is relevant to India. India's educational planners and its University Grants Commission, with scarce resources, see priorities that rank higher than Chinese studies. Nor is there reported to be any pressure to develop specialists on China from those concerned with economic and cultural affairs. Indeed, military fears and political rivalries have probably had a negative impact on India's understanding of China.

In Burma, Thailand, Malaysia, Indonesia, and the Philippines, propinquity and fear of China are complicated by the presence of large numbers of citizens or residents of Chinese origin. In the uncertain relations of these nations with their Chinese minorities, Chinese studies acquire major domestic policy implications. Countries where the Chinese are strongly represented and well known may feel less need to develop formal institutions concerned with Chinese studies. The Chinese "problem" in these nations appears in more immediate domestic terms. As an external force, China seems so overwhelming as to encourage the feeling that only the great powers can handle it in any positive way.

Further afield, in other parts of Asia, and in Africa, Latin America, and the Middle East, there is virtually no academic interest in China. Chinese initiatives in supporting revolutionary causes, spreading propaganda, or offering economic, military, political, and other support desired by local groups or governments do not appear to be sufficient to generate a genuine interest in knowing China. In Chile, for example, revolutionary and economic interests combine to produce some local support for scholarly study of China, but this has not been the case in Cuba. Even countries that have important ties to China, such as Ceylon, Zambia, and Albania, have a very narrow and pragmatic perception of the relationship. They lack sufficient incentives to develop their own independent specialists and facilities to study China for either cultural enrichment or new social and political models.

In the West

In the postwar period, those industrialized countries of the West with strong international interests and well-developed educational institutions have pursued the study of China most actively. Most of these countries had to rebuild their programs after the disruptions of World War II. Because of the radical reduction of their roles in Asia, the priorities for Chinese and Asian studies changed and declined. In both respects, the situation of the United States, with its expanded involvement in Asia, was quite different. But our country needed time to formulate new programs based on a new pattern of incentives. In Western Europe, Canada, and Australia, a combination of economic expectations, desire for more stable international relations, cultural interests, intellectual curiosity, and security considerations has sustained a renewed interest in China. Sweden illustrates a pattern of motivations arising out of early missionary and commercial interests. Cultural concern, with strong royal patronage, is epitomized in the work on early Chinese history and civilization, linguistics, and art of such early Sinologists as Bernhard Karlgren and Oswald Siren, and in the superb collections of the Museum of Far Eastern Antiquities in Stockholm. Sweden's international concerns are expressed in the Institute of Peace Studies. Its intellectual and economic interests are promoted through university programs and through diplomatic and international economic agencies. Czechoslovakia, in contrast to Poland, also provides an example of coalescing postwar cultural, political, and economic interests leading to a notable development of Chinese studies, particularly in modern literature.

In larger countries, the pattern is more complex. In France, England, Germany, and Russia, Sinological studies acquired in the nineteenth century an honored, if still secondary, place in the broader field of Oriental studies, which developed with the global expansion of European enterprise and empire. These countries have useful collections of classical Chinese materials, a few established university chairs, and a body of scholarly publications on Chinese civilization.

In Great Britain, the traditional interest has survived but has not flourished. However, newer programs concerned with modern China have developed at the so-called Hayter centers and elsewhere. They reflect the awareness of the growing interrelation of all major countries. Still, interest and support for work on China clearly has a lower priority than work on many other areas of the non-Western world, particularly parts of the former empire. Several knowledgeable observers feel that only a major growth in Chinese-British economic relations will lead to an expansion of Chinese studies.

However, because of continuing political and economic interests in Asia and particularly because of the delicate position of Hong Kong, the British Government maintains training facilities with extremely high standards to prepare a small number of specialists. A few small programs meet practical requirements—military, political, and economic—and also preserve the nation's academic and scholarly footing in the field. Quality, professionalism, and élitism tend to mark this effort. The scope of the programs fails to satisfy some politically oriented student groups who want to learn about revolutionary systems, as well as some intellectuals and planners concerned with global issues and problems of development in non-Western countries.

Such views, however, are unlikely to prevail in view of severe economic constraints and limited public or official concern with China. The failure to develop and mobilize social scientists to work on China indicates China's modest place in British intellectual and national concern.

Since World War II, the educational system in France, which had a long and distinguished prewar classical tradition of Chinese studies, has tried to meet the interests of substantial numbers of students, largely through establishing Chinese-language courses. Political interest, economic relations, and student exchanges with Peking have had remarkably little influence in expanding and deepening scholarly work on China, past or present. This situation may change with the reorganization of the French university system.

In Germany, an effort to redress postwar neglect was energetically undertaken in the mid-1960's, partly the result of the developing commercial relations between China and Germany and also of a growing appreciation of the implications of the Sino-Soviet conflict for Germany. With the encouragement of private foundations, including the Ford Foundation, the Germans are now embarked on a major and systematic expansion of Chinese studies, particularly as they relate to modern problems. Economic and political motives, building on traditional Sinological interests and resources, may bring German scholarship rapidly to the forefront in Europe.

Developments during the past decade are likely to produce a rapid and somewhat belated expansion of Chinese studies in the Soviet Union. The reasons are basically political and military. Chinese competition within revolutionary movements and the Third World, plus fear of Chinese territorial and military intentions, underlie the Soviet Union's efforts to augment its Sinological studies with serious systematic study of contemporary China. In the scholarly sphere, this new emphasis is exemplified by the founding in 1966 of the Institute of the Far East in the Academy of Sciences, a new training and research effort by the Institute, and the national effort to gain access to scholarly resources throughout Asia and the West.

In countries with highly centralized control over information, education, and scholarly research, the political leadership determines the direction and scope of the effort to understand another country. This can be highly focused, as in the Soviet Union, or more diffuse, as in Czechoslovakia.

The United States

In the United States, the underlying interests and motives that support Chinese studies are not simple to isolate and define. Loose coordination of government and scholarly programs in the United States makes a striking contrast to most other countries, where training and research on

China depend upon centralized allocations of resources and where limited resources prohibit duplication.

Variety and flexibility have been encouraged in the United States because higher education draws upon many sources for support. State legislatures and private agencies have supported many programs of national and international dimensions rather than demonstrable local utility. In other countries, few private donors and local educational bodies devote substantial funds for the study of remote countries or international affairs, which are usually regarded as matters of national rather than regional concern. Exceptions appear in Canada and West Germany.

The U.S. Government, with its strong security and political concerns, has established its own institutions for training specialists and conducting research on China. Apart from crucial Federal fellowship and language-training support under the National Defense Education Act of 1958, embracing a score of languages and areas not well known to Americans and neglected in the educational system, the federal government has had no important role in shaping university programs. The primary impetus behind expanding Chinese studies came from broad interests focused in foundations and universities. In a few states, tax funds are increasingly providing some support.

There is no doubt, however, that China's recent and projected actions have ranked high in attracting support to Chinese studies. The primary justification, for example, for federal fellowship and language support was the need to train specialists to serve the national interest. At the same time, training and research in China's traditional culture, and more recently in the experimental social and economic strategies of the mainland government, have been supported by a wide range of intellectual and cultural interests. Although still constricted, the result is more diversity in American programs and research on China than anywhere outside the Chinese cultural sphere. While economic and commercial motives have had little influence thus far in focusing interest on China, groups with an international outlook, including businessmen, are taking a greater interest in China as American policies of containment are relaxed and prospects of trade with China increase.

The study of China has benefited, therefore, from broad support by government, foundations, and university leaders. Its place in the academic system was notably improved by the decision of the Ford Foundation a decade ago to give Chinese studies special attention. China's uncertain but prospectively large role in world politics sustained this effort. However, changes in the American sense of threat, unexpected developments in China, and shifting views about the U.S. role in world affairs raise serious questions about continued support for the field, especially if support for international studies as a whole continues to decline.

II. The Initial Period of Chinese Studies in the United States

Thus far, the range and depth, if not the diversity, of American scholarly and public interest in China have been limited. The study of China could yield far larger returns. China is not only a unique repository of human experience, but also a remarkable social laboratory. Urbanization, public health, ecological and population trends, educational and industrial strategies—all have a special instructive dimension because of their Chinese environment. The Chinese experience must have value, positive or negative, to everyone concerned about the future of the world.

Before considering the resources now available in the United States for understanding China, it is important to note the way Chinese studies have developed in this country and the unique problems facing the field.

American education and research on China have a long way to go before they provide a balanced view of the world scene. This perspective is urgently needed today. China's modern revolution has become a major focus of social experimentation and of international tension and concern. American studies of China are still vastly inferior in grasp and sophistication to our studies of Greece and Rome, medieval and modern Europe, the British Commonwealth,

Japan, or even the Soviet Union. The comparative under-development of American studies of China is due to an unfortunate combination of factors.

One is the linguistic barrier that separates China from all other countries. Neighboring lands like Japan, Korea, and Vietnam that borrowed the Chinese characters for writing combined them with a phonetic system capable of assimilating foreign words by writing down their sound just as we do. Only the Chinese bloc of one-fifth to one-quarter of mankind remains cut off behind its peculiar semi-ideographic writing system, into which all foreign words and the ideas they represent must be translated by using the characters already available from China's heritage. Foreign ideas are inevitably somewhat Sinified.

In addition, our studies of China are backward because scholars in China itself have been unable fully to modernize their own Chinese studies. Whereas U.S. studies of Britain, France, or Japan can draw upon native scholarship, in China, the main work of modern critical scholarship is still to be done. In this difficulty, our programs in international education might well take an interest in scholarship on China wherever it may be found.

Chinese studies in the United States, until World War II, were in the shadow of the European tradition, which in turn was founded upon the Chinese classical tradition. The first European sign of independence appeared in 1900 when Edouard Chavannes introduced a course in Chinese history at the Collège de France. Since that time, there has been at first a gradual and then an increasingly rapid development of Chinese studies employing modern methods and incorporating teachers and scholars into Western academic settings.

Prior to the mid-1950's, the almost total lack of interest in China in such fields as politics, economics, sociology, and law forced history into a central place in the development of Chinese studies. Historians, working closely with and sometimes within departments of Chinese or Far Eastern languages and literature, and teachers of language provided the foundations for Chinese studies in this country. In an initial stage, when students need to grasp the total image of a completely alien society, the historical introduction has been indispensable. Moreover, the historians' image and projection of China has become even more valuable as their work has developed sophistication and is increasingly informed by concepts and knowledge from other social scientists.

The main difficulty, however, especially since World War II, has been the inability of history to meet a new range of needs. In early Western encounters with a weak and amorphous China, China's past was the prime fascination. Now the present tends to take center stage. China's economic capacities, political dynamism and power, and social transformations command attention inside and outside of its boundaries. Because of urgent demands from the nonacademic world, deficiencies in our knowledge of those modern-contemporary developments of central interest to social scientists now stand out.

But every part of the field, given its early neglect and its uneven growth, needs development. The strength and future progress of the field lie in its overall coherence. At the same time, there is a basic need to integrate Chinese studies more fully into the network of departments that make up most universities.

A new approach to the study of other countries, developed during and after the war, is the interdisciplinary area program. In a sense, this approach reflected the classical study of the traditional Orient by attempting to cover the totality of a culture. As defined by Wendell C. Bennett in his *Area Studies in American Universities,** this meant an

* New York: Social Science Research Council, 1951.

integrated program that offered at least five pertinent subjects, in addition to competent instruction in the principal
language or languages of a particular area or country.

Area studies were a reaction in part against the "hard-
ening walls between traditional disciplines" and in part
against the neglect of the new countries and peoples entering the world community. As a result, there was a growing
demand for higher education to provide the same comprehensive treatment of China and other non-Western cultures
as of Western civilization.*

Because existing departments in the China field were
Sinological (i.e., traditional or classical) in orientation, social scientists—concerned primarily with the modern world
—took the lead in forming new centers to expand Chinese
studies. These interdisciplinary centers looked to the traditional departments, first for language training, particularly
in its modern spoken form, and secondly for background
courses on the traditional culture.

The essential steps in developing the field have been:
(1) language training; (2) fellowships for students at all
stages of graduate, and some undergraduate, training; (3)
multidisciplinary area courses and field orientation in a
Chinese setting, including the establishment of facilities
abroad; (4) special efforts to train students in the social
sciences for work on China; (5) establishing new teaching
posts relating to China in more university departments;
(6) postdoctoral research grants; (7) special research
facilities and provisions to offset China's inaccessibility;
(8) measures to increase the availability of Chinese publications and research data; (9) support of special projects
and activities, such as bibliographies, research cooperation,
and exchange of information, to increase the efficiency and

---

* The section on area studies owes much to the report of the Commission on International Understanding, *Non-Western Studies in the
Liberal Arts College* (Washington, D.C.: Association of American Colleges, 1964).

sustain the intellectual vitality of students and scholars in the field; (10) strengthening or developing centers at key universities to give coherence to this complex process; and (11) the use of national committees, councils, and associations to provide formal and informal leadership in advancing the enterprise on a national scale.

The results of these efforts since the late 1950's are now manifest, but the fruits are yet to be realized in full. The various elements in the developmental process will be dealt with in subsequent chapters.

III. The Developmental Decade

Prior to World War II, only a few universities, relying on their own resources, supported Chinese studies. During and after the war, American studies of China began to develop their own characteristic methods of instruction and research and their own outlook. With the help of the major foundations, and later of the federal government, teaching posts were established in university departments. Thus, Chinese studies began to infiltrate various disciplines in the humanities and social sciences. This process, which has been uneven, is far from complete. In general, departments of history have been ready to embrace Chinese history. Separate departments of Chinese language and literature have sprung up, with few in close working relation with major departments of Western literature. Whereas anthropology accommodated China during and after the war, sociology has only begun to do so.

Economics departments have, in general, proved difficult to penetrate—partly because their models and methods are often applicable only to developed economies. However, with the growing focus on problems of economic development, China has increasingly become of major theoretical and practical importance. Similarly, political science departments pioneering in comparative politics and international systems analysis have sought to take account of China.

This effort to enlarge the intellectual and disciplinary approach to China met a ready and eager response. The social sciences themselves, in varying degrees, were in the process of change as they coped with problems posed by profound and often violent transformation of economic, political, and social systems in most of the world. Many departments were therefore ready for colleagues qualified to deal with China in relevant disciplinary terms.

Before the war, the American Oriental Society provided an occasional forum for the presentation of Sinological papers. The main body that mobilized a wide variety of Americans, from missionaries to newsmen and scholars interested in contemporary Chinese problems, was the American Council of the international Institute of Pacific Relations, which approached China in a broad Asian context. Its series of monographic studies, its two principal serial publications, *Pacific Affairs* and *Far Eastern Survey*, and its research funds dominated the field. The Rockefeller Foundation was the largest single contributor to the Council, granting $164,400 in the period 1933–45.

With the expansion of academic work during and after the war, the American Oriental Society could no longer meet the growing needs of scholars concerned with East Asia. The Committee on Far Eastern Studies of the American Council of Learned Societies (ACLS), which with Rockefeller Foundation support had promoted training of China specialists prior to the war, encouraged the Far Eastern Association, organized in June, 1941, to publish *The Far Eastern Quarterly*, to transform itself into "an active-membership, learned society with expanded objectives and interests." * This it did at an organizational

* For an account of the founding and transformation of The Far Eastern Association, see *The Far Eastern Quarterly,* VII, 4 (August, 1948), 410–18.

meeting of about 200 scholars held at Columbia University on April 2, 1948. The first annual meeting of the new association was held at Yale a year later.

In the decade that followed, the association—renamed the Association for Asian Studies in 1956—served the professional needs of scholars and others interested in China. The ACLS channeled modest foundation funds to support of research on China and Asia through its Committee on Asian Studies, established in 1958.

During this period, additional universities established area and language programs relating to China, bringing the number up to seventeen by 1958. However, language instruction was still generally weak, and, apart from history, work on China in the social sciences languished. The improvement of linguistic competence in a score of languages, including Chinese, was Congress's primary aim in passing the National Defense Education Act of 1958. Language and related background studies took on new life with funds provided by NDEA for instruction, preparation of teaching materials, and related research.

At the same time, foundation support permitted the development and expansion of undergraduate and, primarily, graduate training in modern history and the social sciences at a number of institutions, most of which had NDEA centers offering complementary support. Foundation support was provided over a long period of time for a variety of coordinate activities and programs in order to achieve the training and research competence necessary for sound scholarship relating to China. Training of more scholars and teachers was the first priority. Hence, the bulk of the support went to graduate schools. Scholarly research was underwritten to raise the level of knowledge and bring the number and quality of publications up to prevailing academic and scholarly standards.

The development of more courses followed, as well as the expansion of work on China to new institutions. The process was quite gradual in most disciplines. It was controlled partly by the institutions themselves and partly by the selective allocation of new funds by the federal government and by foundations. Supporting agencies, public and private, were agreed that quality rather than quantity should govern this stage of growth in a field as complex, important, and vulnerable to political misuse as the study of China.

As work on East Asia became more specialized, sophisticated, and concerned with modern developments, the myths about a uniform Oriental or East Asian universe crumbled. The distinctive problems and complexities of modern China, Japan, and Korea were too great to be encompassed by serious students; both country and disciplinary specialization was essential. China, therefore, came under scholarly scrutiny from varied perspectives. Centers and programs of Chinese study developed at many universities, and committees and projects relating to China appeared with various institutional sponsors. The Ford Foundation took the lead in a major developmental program in 1959–60 that rapidly strengthened and broadened resources and work on modern China, particularly in the social sciences, at a number of major universities. In the meantime, the Institute of Pacific Relations, caught in political controversy, came to an end.

Expansion in the field led to the establishment of organizations and committees to promote new interests and to manage growing specialized resources. No longer could one or two organizations accommodate these proliferating activities and handle the problems both of traditional Sinologists and of specialists on modern and contemporary China, nor cope with both the humanities and the social sciences.

The critical academic problem for producing and sustaining the new specialists on modern and contemporary China was to gain inclusion and support within the regular departments. Every discipline or group of disciplines—each with its own requirements, style, prejudices, and degree of accessibility to new concerns—required special approaches and efforts.

If the study of traditional China in our system tends to be integrated and culture-oriented and to highlight the unique, the study of modern China, on the other hand, has been fragmented among the various social-science disciplines. Disciplinary interests are primary; knowledge of language and area prerequisite tools. The study of China is expected to increase understanding of human behavior and of society as a whole. At the same time, disciplinary perspectives are expected to make essential contributions to an understanding of what is distinctive and characteristic about China. Thus, the study of modern and contemporary China has been an interdepartmental enterprise involving language as a tool and history as a bridge between past and present. Within this framework comes concentration on political science, economics, anthropology, sociology, geography, and such professional specializations as law, education, and medicine. The importance of linking specialists on China to their professional colleagues in the disciplines led to the formation of a number of committees and the organization of specialized projects and conferences.

When the Ford Foundation embarked on its major program to develop the study of modern and contemporary China, it decided to give substantial support to four major university centers where significant work on contemporary China could, it appeared, be rapidly advanced. These were Harvard, Columbia, California (Berkeley), and the University of Washington. All had well-developed centers for the study of East Asia, significant library holdings, and centers for the study of the Soviet Union with resources to support scholarly work on Communist China. In addition, the Foundation saw opportunities to encourage other institutions, such as The Hoover Institution on War, Revolution, and Peace, Stanford, Yale, Cornell, and the University of California (Los Angeles), as well as individuals at universities and colleges that lacked major institutional resources.

Foundation officials dealt directly with institutions in working out grants. They felt, however, that neither individuals nor individual institutions could achieve the requisite balanced and comprehensive development of the field. The idea of organizing a committee to develop a cooperative national effort on the model of the Joint Committee on Slavic Studies already had been discussed by a panel at the annual meeting of the Association for Asian Studies held in Washington in 1958. This possibility, and the need to discover the views of representative scholars in the field, led the Foundation to sponsor a gathering of leading specialists on China.

The Gould House Conference on Studies of Contemporary China that resulted was held near New York in June, 1959, the first meeting of its kind in ten years. It proposed that a special national committee be set up "to promote the study of contemporary China." This was the genesis the same year of the Joint Committee on Contemporary China (JCCC) of the ACLS and the Social Science Research Council (SSRC). A major goal of the JCCC was to gain acceptance for Chinese studies and to place responsibility within a whole panorama of American institutions and bodies concerned with training, research, professional activities, and public affairs. The result of these and related efforts has been to reduce, if not eliminate, the isolation of Chinese studies and the neglect of China in such fields of present concern as arms control, international security affairs, law, and trade.

The JCCC, administered by the SSRC, has been entrusted for twelve years with the responsibility for spending, directly and through its subcommittees and related committees, more than $2 million. It has had a role in starting many other enterprises, such as the Committee on the Economy of China, the Committee on Exchanges with Asian Institutions; the American Historical Association's program in diplomatic history on American–East Asian relations; and the Association of Research Libraries' Center for Chinese Research Materials. It has also helped expand the work of other bodies through endorsement or support, such as a microfilm project of the Library of Congress and microfilms for the Midwest Inter-Library Center (now the Center for Research Libraries). Altogether it has helped to channel to various enterprises an additional $1.5 million for the further development of the field. Support has come from many sources, but the Ford Foundation has provided the bulk of the funds, more than $3 million.

Twenty-four scholars, from thirteen institutions, have served on the JCCC since its founding. Altogether thirty-eight scholars have served on the Committee and its subcommittees. Their service has meant a considerable sacrifice of time, for members receive no honoraria, and forgo the opportunity to apply for funds from the committees they serve.

In summary, between 1960–61 and 1968–69, the JCCC's activities included 115 grants to support the research of 103 scholars; sponsorship of 30 research conferences and seminars, relating to virtually all the social sciences, with 662 participants from every part of the world; the publication or prospective publication of two major guides to research data; support for a dictionary of political, legal, and administrative items; and publication of a substantial body of research monographs, symposium volumes, and scholarly studies of modern and contemporary China. The special emphasis of its program of research grants has made research possible for a large number of scholars at institutions with limited resources.

The main thrust of the Committee's effort, both officially

and through its members, has been to legitimize, promote, and "domesticate" work on modern China, both in training and research. Its efforts have taken account of the panoramic range of scholarly disciplines and institutions in this country—including libraries, associations, colleges and universities, regional facilities, research agencies, and professional bodies.

Two related committees, administered by ACLS, have at the same time supported, expanded, and fostered the intellectual vitality of Sinologists. The first of these was the Joint Committee on Asian Studies, which offered grants for postdoctoral research on China, Japan, Korea, and South and Southeast Asia.* By 1964, there was a strong feeling among specialists on traditional China that their area also benefited from developmental and cooperative undertakings.This led to the founding that year of the ACLS Committee on Studies of Chinese Civilization. Using funds from the Ford Foundation, it has organized conferences and fostered projects on such aspects of Imperial China as governmental institutions, thought and religion, art, literature, and the Sung dynasty.

From 1959 to 1969, the Joint Committee on Asian Studies awarded fifty-six research grants. The Committee on Studies of Chinese Civilization has organized or sponsored conferences on Ming dynasty government, Ming thought, Taoism, Chinese literary genres, and social thought and institutional change in China from 750 to 1350, in which eighty-nine scholars have participated. These two committees and their subcommittees concerned with Imperial China have from 1958 to 1969 enlisted forty-two scholars as members.

Altogether more than seventy-five scholars in Chinese

---

* Following reorganization in 1969, work on China was continued by the Joint Committee on East Asian Studies, a successor to the Joint Committee on Asian Studies.

studies have served on the three major grants and developmental committees of the two councils. In working terms, progress and achievements in the field, as well as its shortcomings, can in some measure be attributed to them. The vigor and developmental enterprise of the committees has really depended, however, upon a much smaller number of scholars who have initiated, planned, and overseen the various activities sponsored by these committees.

There have been, in addition, a number of committees with more highly focused mandates, some already mentioned in connection with the JCCC. The SSRC has administered the Committee on the Economy of China (organized in 1961), the Committee on Exchanges with Asian Institutions (founded in 1961), the Joint Committee on the Foreign Area Fellowship Program (established in 1962), and (with the ACLS) has administered the Joint Committee on Sino-American Cooperation in the Humanities and Social Sciences (formed in 1966).

The National Academy of Sciences–National Research Council has also helped to support activities related to China. Its U.S. Committee on Sino-American Science Cooperation (founded in 1962) cooperates with the Academia Sinica on the development of graduate training in natural sciences in Taiwan. On a wider basis, the Academy (with the ACLS and SSRC) administers a Joint Committee on Scholarly Communication with Mainland China, established in 1966, that seeks opportunities to open communications with scientists and scholars in mainland China.*

Another range of related activities is sponsored by

---

* In addition to the above organizations, the Liaison Committee on the Study of Contemporary China was organized in 1965. With the support of a five-year grant from the Ford Foundation, this Committee has been fostering international cooperation in training and research on twentieth-century China, working to relate American scholars with their colleagues in Britain, France, Germany, Australia, Japan, and elsewhere.

professional associations and organizations. Although the primary function of the disciplinary and area associations of scholars is to sponsor publications, meetings, and other activities of professional concern to their particular field, they also have sponsored projects, programs, and conferences in Asian studies. The Association for Asian Studies' membership of 4,000 is so diverse that it recently established area councils better to meet their different interests, ranging from Japan to Afghanistan. One is an elected China and Inner Asia Regional Council of nine members. It has yet to define its role beyond developing appropriate panels for its constituents at annual meetings and sponsoring other meetings. China figures very prominently in some of the Association's established committees—such as those on East Asian languages and East Asian libraries and the Committee on Buddhist Studies. The Association earlier sponsored a series of conferences on Chinese thought under the direction of a committee appointed for this purpose and, since 1964, has sponsored the Chinese Materials and Research Aids Service Center in Taiwan under a separate board of directors.

The American Oriental Society continues to provide a forum for scholars concerned with classical studies of China and has on several occasions coordinated its annual meetings with those of the Association of Asian Studies. Other associations also play a role. The American Geographical Society has a Committee on Chinese Geographical Literature. The American Political Science Association has a panel on comparative Communism that takes account of China. The Modern Language Association has undertaken projects related to the teaching of Chinese and Japanese. The American Society for International Law has sponsored conferences relating to Chinese law. Other groups, noted above, also have assisted in supporting the development of the field, such as the American Historical Association and the Association of Research Libraries.

The panoply of institutions and committees involved in developing Chinese studies has recently produced questions and complaints. Although the dissatisfactions expressed vary widely, most can be grouped according to four major areas of concern.

First, there is the division within the field, variously described as between scholars of Imperial China and those of modern China, Sinologists and scholars of modern China, Sinologists and the social scientists, or area specialists and disciplinary specialists. In universities, the Sinologists, classicists, and area specialists are often grouped in a single department; professionally, these scholars tend to rely on the American Oriental Society and the Association of Asian Studies. The scholars of modern China and the disciplinary specialists, on the other hand, usually belong to various departments but are often brought together in interdisciplinary centers; professionally, they tend to rely on the Social Science Research Council and the American Council of Learned Societies, as well as their disciplinary associations, to forward their concerns with China.

Second, there have been charges that the foundations have sought to impose their views and priorities on universities and the Chinese field as a whole. Some of the critics object to the emphasis on the modern and contemporary, viewing it as the success of one group of scholars in the so-called game of academic politics. Others object they have known too little of the procedures involved in preparing proposals for foundation support and of the actual operation of committees and institutions.

A third area of criticism, related to the second, alleges domination of the field by a small group of scholars. A particular target has been the Joint Committee on Contemporary China. This charge relates also to a fourth area of criticism that goes beyond the scope of Chinese studies, concerning as it does the emergence of political groupings within the professional scholarly community, such as ethnic minorities, anti-war, and anti-establishment groups. The implications of all these divisions and strains will be considered later in connection with the problems and prospects that face Chinese studies.

IV. Language and Area Training

Knowledge of language is the necessary base for the study of any society. Prerequisite to teaching Chinese effectively in an academic setting is an understanding of the language through linguistic research, the preparation of teaching aids, and curriculum development.

The teaching of Chinese in the United States dates back to courses at Harvard in 1870. Prior to World War II, Chinese language courses, offered at only a handful of universities such as Harvard, Columbia, Chicago, University of California (Berkeley), and Pennsylvania, were largely devoted to teaching classical Chinese in order to train Sinologists. The second stage began with the wartime need to prepare large numbers of Americans to speak Chinese and Japanese. New training methods to speed the process of learning were developed, which stressed speaking the language and reading the modern vernacular. Yale University, through a series of contracts with the Air Force, became the leading center for the preparation of this new type of Chinese-language specialist. Columbia and Harvard pioneered in Chinese area study.

Following a decade of deferred growth, a third period began in 1959 after the passage of the National Defense Education Act, as noted earlier. Although the act helped establish and strengthen language and area centers for work on world areas where the United States was adjudged critically short of specialists (China was one of six), language instruction was stressed, with special fellowships for graduate work and funds for linguistic research and curriculum development.

Since then, it has been suggested that, despite the special challenges the Chinese language presents, the teaching of Chinese has not been notable for experimental use of new techniques and technologies. Various reasons are cited: The fact that language training has usually been the responsibility of departments with a classical background or orientation; the heavy dependence on Chinese-language instructors without linguistic training; and the separation of East Asian language departments from the main stream of modern language work.

Moreover, classical documentary and literary Chinese is so disjunctured from the modern spoken and written form of the language, both necessary for many types of scholarly pursuits, as to lay a double language burden on both departments of instruction and students. At present, however, a few efforts are under way to develop radically new methods of teaching Chinese.

Only about 8 per cent of the 2,400 institutions of higher education in the United States provide Chinese language instruction; the total enrollment in such courses (about 5,000 compared to Russian-language enrollment of about 30,000) represents less than one student out of 1,300. Nonetheless, there has been a marked growth in the number of college and university students studying Chinese. Enrollment increased from 1,844 in 1960 to 5,061 in 1968 (see Appendix I), when something of a plateau was reached. In addition, between 150 and 200 American secondary schools provide some instruction in Chinese to between 2,000 and 3,000 students. (See Appendix II.)

AMERICAN COLLEGES AND UNIVERSITIES WITH STUDENT
ENROLLMENTS IN CHINESE LANGUAGE COURSES

	No. of Institutions *			*Enrollment*	
			NDEA		
	Undergraduate	*Graduate*	*Centers*	*Undergraduate*	*Graduate*
1965	78	31	19	2,561	798
1968	108	35	28	4,090	971

* The figures for institutions offering undergraduate courses include
those offering graduate work. Thus column one overlaps column two.

Most of the leading institutions receive NDEA support.
In 1968, somewhat less than a third of the undergraduate
students of Chinese language (1,157) were in NDEA
centers, but the bulk of the graduate students (662) were.
Many of the smaller programs are dependent upon one or
two instructors, often part-time and partly trained native
Chinese speakers, whose availability sometimes is for-
tuitous. These institutions often have no regular language-
linguistic departments related to regular programs in Chinese studies; rather, they provide language courses to meet
local demands. Enrollment can be fairly large at institutions introducing ethnic or minority studies or enrolling
numerous students of Chinese background.

At a time when student interest in Chinese has been
growing, there has been a sharp reduction in Federal support for such studies. The quota of graduate fellowships for
1971–72 is set at 180 for all of East Asia—a sharp cutback from 1970–71 when more than 300 fellowships were
awarded. At the same time, the funds for training and
modest research on language teaching has been entirely
eliminated. Table I indicates what this means for students
and institutions.

The extension of undergraduate Chinese instruction is
producing change in the field. In 1955, virtually no undergraduates studied the language. Graduate schools therefore,
at heavy cost, had to provide introductory language courses
and compensate for the enormous amount of time it took

TABLE I

INSTITUTIONS PARTICIPATING IN THE NDEA TITLE VI EAST ASIAN PROGRAM

Institutions (* Denotes NDEA Center, 1969–70)	1968 Student Enrollments		1969–70 Quotas for Graduate Fellowships (NDFL) in East Asian Languages (Chinese, Japanese, Korean, etc.)	1971–72 NDFL Quotas	1969 Allocation of NDEA Funds for East Asian Centers
	Under-graduate	Graduate			
*Arizona	38	10	3	3	$ 55,000
*Brown	20	11	1	1	28,240
*Bucknell	NA	NA			23,000
*California (Berkeley)	138	43	24	14	100,000
California (Davis)	48	6	1	1	
California (Los Angeles)	156	6			
*Chicago	92	49	3	2	53,000
*Colorado	78	—	20	9	53,000
*Columbia	120	111	52	25	139,000
*Cornell	43	6(?)	7	4	62,000
*Dartmouth	14	—			36,000
*Fordham	NA	—			35,000
George Washington	101	?	3	1	
Georgetown	29	10	1	1	
*Harvard	47(?)	66(?)	53	26	134,900
*Hawaii	170	88		2	82,650
Indiana	108	40	6	5	
*Illinois	59	—	3	4	38,000

*Iowa	168	6	2	1	42,500
*Kansas	54	—	4	3	58,650
*Manhattanville	11	—			21,850
*Michigan	88	81	31	16	68,000
*Michigan State (Oakland)	40	6			29,350
Minnesota	45	9	3	2	21,500
*Oberlin	28	—			
Pennsylvania	78	8(?)	4	3	47,250
*Pittsburgh	59	2	2	1	50,000
*Princeton	22	9(?)		8	25,000
*Rochester	24	—			
*Southern California	87	27	3	1	58,620
*Stanford	42	42	15	10	
*Texas	46	—	2	1	43,000
*Washington	40	42(?)	27	16	73,940
*Washington U. (St Louis)	36	1	3	3	
Wisconsin	87	59	6	5	
*Yale	25	20	20	9	53,200
Totals	2241	758	299	177	$1,432,650

NOTES: 1. Question mark after number indicates use of the 1965 figure because the 1968 enrollment is unreported.

2. If the University of California (Santa Barbara), Claremont College, and Ohio State are added to the 1971–72 fellowship list, the total comes to 180.

graduate students to acquire an elementary working knowledge of the language. Although precise figures are unavailable, an increasing number of students are now being admitted to graduate schools with two to four years of undergraduate work in Chinese.

However, even if Chinese is taught at hundreds of colleges and if, as in the case of Russian, 30,000 rather than 4,000 undergraduate students learn something of the language each year, it still will not be feasible to impose a significant language prerequisite for admission to graduate training. There will be continued need to encourage those students who defer their career choices to pursue work in this complex and only developing field.

Despite the fact that the first two years of Chinese language study are not credited toward an advanced degree, for some time to come, graduate schools will have to offer the entire range of language instruction. One immediate consequence of undergraduate study of Chinese, however, is the need for graduate schools to develop more advanced courses in the disciplines using Chinese-language materials. Standards are raised, but so are costs.

The development of programs in Chinese tailored to the departmental requirements of the social sciences has meant a drop in language standards. For social scientists, language is primarily a tool to enter into the social, political, economic, scientific, and psychological realm of the Chinese. Language and area training are secondary. Intense competition, the pace and structure of specialized graduate training, and a narrow professionalism create a situation in which most of our graduate students are neither required nor inspired to gain full competence in the language and a working penetration of the Chinese cultural setting.

For many purposes, such advanced scholarship is not necessary for Americans, any more than it is necessary in our mass educational system for secondary school teachers or even college teachers to have the capacity for original work. It might be argued, therefore, that most of the graduate students preparing for undergraduate teaching in the disciplines do not need a full mastery of Chinese. Success in their future occupation will depend not on their ability to work in and on China and the Chinese, but on their ability to translate, interpret, and transmit to others knowledge and perceptions about China. Even if this argument is accepted, however, the need still remains for a corps of American scholars capable of basic, competent, professionally rigorous, and original work on China.

As in European studies, advanced students preparing for scholarly careers relating to another society should have part of their training in a Chinese university. The social sciences are largely undeveloped in Chinese universities, academic standards are low, and the educational environment is not generally propitious for the foreign student. It is not possible, then, to send our students to Chinese institutions, as we send them to French, German, Italian, Spanish, Swedish, and even Russian institutions. Consequently, our best students and the leaders among the present generation of younger scholars who are not Chinese-born must have longer and broader training. Because of the acute shortage of college and university faculty during the past decade, we impressed too many of our graduate students into teaching before they had completed their training and won their degrees. While such measures are no longer necessary, both these young scholars and their successors must have the opportunity, on a competitive basis, to continue their studies.

A large percentage of advanced students now spend a year in a Chinese setting, working on language and research. The principal facility for Americans is the invaluable Inter-University Program of Chinese Language Studies in Taipei (described later in this chapter). Without it, a substantial proportion of the 412 men and women receiving doctorates between 1960 and 1970 would have lacked any exposure to language training in a Chinese setting. But more needs to be done. Perhaps students should achieve real mastery of the language before embarking on disciplinary work. Teachers and students have suggested that the Taipei center or some other center be used to prepare students for a "total" immersion—or "conditioning"—in a Chinese setting, or to prepare students for study in a Chinese university. The time seems right to undertake some pilot projects that will enable a few students to test various routes to a mastery of language in such places as Taiwan, Hong Kong, and Singapore. Their experiences would help us to plan improvements in our present institutionalized procedures of language training.

A complementary approach to the problem of language is through improved teaching methods. Interest in Chinese linguistics has produced a substantial corps of specialists; more than 30 received doctorates between 1960 and 1969. The Chinese Linguistics Project at Princeton University has helped some of these specialists to work together. A further step would be to combine the talents of the linguists with the requirements of working language instructors and thus experiment with new methods of teaching and using language for a wide variety of scholarly and professional needs. Because linguistic interests are common to all countries with programs on China, the conditions for broad international cooperation seem particularly promising. Indeed, it has already started.

School Chinese, like school French, may be sufficient to open new perspectives and add some knowledge. Neither is sufficient for creative scholarship. For these serious purposes, language has to be a fluid medium of discourse and understanding. Because China among the great civilizations has always been the most distant and distinctively different from the West, our scholarly effort still has far to go in setting appropriate standards and goals. Hence, we have been, and for some time to come will continue to be, dependent on scholars of Chinese origin to help us maintain certain standards.

Disciplines, Programs, and Centers

More than half of the scholars now working on China received their doctorates between 1960 and 1969. The number of doctoral degrees has steadily mounted from 17 in 1960 to 68 in 1969. Altogether, as noted earlier; they number more than 400. Almost two-thirds were trained at nine universities. About one-third of them (145) are Chinese who migrated to this country for their advanced training. (See Appendix III.)

Although fifty-six universities awarded one or more degrees for doctoral dissertations concerned with China (see Appendix IV), many do not have programs of Chinese studies. For example, departments of economics at many universities, such as Alabama, have allowed a Chinese student to do his dissertation on some aspect of the Chinese economy, using Chinese sources. A similar practice has been followed in other fields, including religion, education, journalism, and political science. Eliminating such institutions, as of 1969, there were twenty-three universities that, based on their awards of doctoral degrees and their academic resources, offered regular doctoral programs in Chinese studies. They are listed on page 56.

The number of institutions has grown from 12 in 1964, to 20 in 1967, to 23 in 1969. Not all of them have a fully developed program of multidisciplinary area studies relating to China. If this is defined, following Wendell Bennett, to mean instruction in the language plus five disciplines, nine or ten universities qualify.

The universities that made an early start have remained in the lead for a variety of reasons: library resources; faculty and programs that attracted students; large fellowship funds and fellowship quotas; proportionately large NDEA funds for further training, as well as large foundation support. This concentration of resources led in turn to the establishment of research centers which then ob-

Number of Ph.D.'s Awarded in Chinese Studies, by University, 1960–69

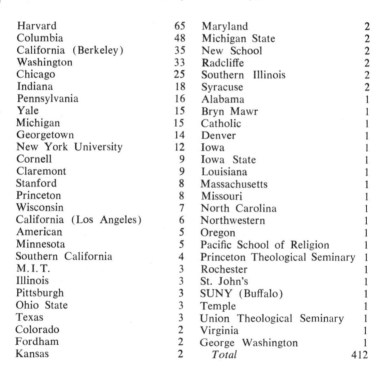

Harvard	65	Maryland	2
Columbia	48	Michigan State	2
California (Berkeley)	35	New School	2
Washington	33	Radcliffe	2
Chicago	25	Southern Illinois	2
Indiana	18	Syracuse	2
Pennsylvania	16	Alabama	1
Yale	15	Bryn Mawr	1
Michigan	15	Catholic	1
Georgetown	14	Denver	1
New York University	12	Iowa	1
Cornell	9	Iowa State	1
Claremont	9	Louisiana	1
Stanford	8	Massachusetts	1
Princeton	8	Missouri	1
Wisconsin	7	North Carolina	1
California (Los Angeles)	6	Northwestern	1
American	5	Oregon	1
Minnesota	5	Pacific School of Religion	1
Southern California	4	Princeton Theological Seminary	1
M.I.T.	3	Rochester	1
Illinois	3	St. John's	1
Pittsburgh	3	SUNY (Buffalo)	1
Ohio State	3	Temple	1
Texas	3	Union Theological Seminary	1
Colorado	2	Virginia	1
Fordham	2	George Washington	1
Kansas	2	*Total*	412

tained funds and attracted visiting scholars and research associates. Undergraduate studies, drawing on the resources of the graduate programs, expanded rapidly. A substantial community of students and scholars developed.

Each of the five largest centers offers more than seventy-five courses in language and at least five disciplines relating to China, has at least fifteen faculty members working on China, has both undergraduate and graduate programs, is within a major university setting, and has strong library and research resources.

Like the universities, the disciplines that were strong in the earlier period have remained strong. Of the 412 doctoral degrees awarded in the developmental decade, history remains far ahead of all other fields with 149. If language (34) and literature (49) are treated as one, as they often are, this field stands second with 83 degrees awarded. Political science is third with 75, followed by anthropology (27), economics (21), art (11), geography (10), religion (8), education (8), law (4), sociology (4), demography (2), philosophy (2), library science (2), and agricultural economics, music, archaeology, business administration, and history of science (1 each). (See Appendix III.)

A very large proportion—say 350—of these recent degree recipients have joined university and college faculties. As a result, graduate programs doubled and tripled, as noted above, and graduate centers grew larger and stronger.

While there is insufficient data to draw a reliable map of Chinese studies, its general configuration is clear. Approximately 2,500 high school students and 5,000 college and university students are now studying the Chinese language. Reports from NDEA centers provide further information on which to base some rough conclusions. In Chinese studies during the ten years between 1959 and 1969, about 1,700 B.A.'s and 1,000 M.A.'s were awarded in addition to the 412 Ph.D.'s. Because the lower degrees are not all terminal, the total number of students receiving more than two years of language training at these centers is somewhat less, say about 2,300. Including students at other institutions, the total comes to about 3,000.

Faculty members devoting all or a substantial part of their time to Chinese studies now probably number between 550 and 600. Of these, about 200 devote full or part time to language instruction, and 350 to 400 to other courses on China. There are perhaps another 50 to 100 Chinese language assistants employed part time. These faculty members belong to more than 100 institutions which provide language instruction, and perhaps another 50 institutions which do not.

Despite a major effort to strengthen work in the social sciences (other than history), the record to date is not altogether encouraging. When the disciplinary distribution of students currently enrolled in graduate schools becomes available, it may show some redress of imbalances in the field. Informal reports from a number of institutions do not suggest, however, that any major shift is taking place.

Significant progress has occurred only in political science. A number of anthropologists doing field work in Taiwan and among overseas Chinese have been recruited to the field. Sociology and economics have been gravely handicapped by lack of access to mainland China for field work and data. Should China become accessible to Americans and usable data made available, the weakness of the social sciences, particularly in economics and sociology, will be acutely apparent.*

Of the new generation of scholars, almost half (174) have been concerned with pre-1900 China. There continue

* A large number of doctoral dissertations written by Chinese students and dealing with Taiwan have not been included in our tallies because they treat the economy, institutional development, or external relations of Taiwan as an independent system unrelated to mainland China.

to be differences within the field about the relative stress that should be given to the past and the present. History's central place in the development of Chinese studies sets the field off from the development of Russian studies, for example, where social sciences have been central. Because Chinese civilization is unique, most scholars have felt that history provided the most satisfactory introduction to China.

This view and the related curricular approach to China, however, were adopted before the Communists came to power. Some scholars and students feel that interdisciplinary programs might now be refocused to introduce America to China through its present-day social realities rather than through its past great tradition. The bulk of China's people have not only neglected but rejected the past. So it is not at all clear that an understanding of the past contributes directly to an American understanding of China today, nor that specialists on the Imperial era and tradition are especially equipped to shape the American encounter with China in its revolutionary present. There is a danger of reading the past into the present, just as there is a danger of reading the present into the past. It appears clear, however, that American isolation from mainland China, dependence on Taiwan, and the strength of old habits and orientations, especially in language and literature, have led to a loss of "feel" for contemporary China.

Fellowships

The growing number of graduate students specializing in China resulted directly from increased fellowship support that attracted students and permitted them to embark on a course of study that takes two to three years longer than the period required in less demanding areas. This process of recruitment and training began in 1952 with *until what year?*

the inauguration of the Ford Foundation Foreign Area Fellowship Program (FAFP), administered since 1962 by the Social Science Research Council. It was sharply accelerated in 1958 by the National Defense Foreign Language Fellowships (NDFL). These programs were supplemented by the NDEA Title IV research fellowships, Fulbright Fellowships administered by the State Department (State), grants under the Mutual Educational and Cultural Exchange Act (Fulbright-Hayes) administered by the Department of Health, Education and Welfare, and a few graduate student research grants from the National Science Foundation.

In the period between 1959 and 1970, a total of 1,796 NDFL predoctoral fellowship awards were made to about 600 students of Chinese. This program has been the major source of support for graduate students in the United States. For predoctoral study and research abroad, primarily in Taiwan and Hong Kong, the FAFP has been the major source of support. Three hundred and seventy-five awards have been made to 203 students of Chinese between 1952 and 1970, 73 of whom received awards in the period 1952–1958. By 1968, 48 students had received graduate fellowships under the Fulbright and Fulbright-Hayes programs, 39 for work in Taiwan and 9 for research in Hong Kong.

These fellowships, totaling about 2,200 awards and an expenditure of about $10.8 million, represent something between a third and a half of the total support provided graduate students in the Chinese field during the past twelve years. The remainder came through university fellowships, student aid and work programs, Ford Foundation grants administered by various university centers, and a large number of smaller fellowship programs. Because the major fellowship programs are open only to American and Canadian citizens or permanent residents, considerable support from other sources has been used for foreign, primarily Chinese, students. A relatively small proportion of the training costs of either American or foreign students is paid for by the students themselves.

It is evident that without special fellowship programs, such as the NDFL and the FAFP, few students would have been willing or able to embark on six to eight years of graduate study when in most disciplines one could earn a doctorate, with likelihood of continuous fellowship support, in three to five years. Universities could not make such heavy investments to benefit a new, small field like Chinese where employment opportunities in teaching and government and business were limited.

However, with special outside funds to pick up the extra costs, the universities have given customary levels of fellowship support for students working on China.

The NDFL and other government fellowship programs appear to be reaching an end, and the FAFP has been cut back.* Graduate studies in Chinese will thus be gravely affected. There will be a rapid reduction in students entering the field. Of those who do, few will have the opportunity to spend the essential time in Asia. Programs and faculty time will probably be refocused from graduate to undergraduate training. Should this country develop intensive undergraduate programs in Chinese, on the European model, there would be, some might argue, compensation for the reduction in graduate programs.

Two problems would still remain, however: redressing weaknesses in the field, and helping students who have already made a major commitment of time and energy to Chinese studies to complete their training. Of the 900 to

* At the time Professor Lindbeck wrote these words, the NDFL and other governmental fellowship programs had been cut back from $15.3 million for 1970 to $6 million for 1971, and the projected funding for 1972 was zero. However, thanks mainly to pressure from the universities, 1972 funding has been restored to the 1970 level ($15.3 million).

1,000 graduate students now in course, a substantial number merit one to four more years of fellowship support to complete their training. Many of them are prepared to do excellent work and make an important contribution to the future development of a field that is undergoing drastic change.

Finally, it would be foolish to allow Chinese studies to decline at a time when China's involvement with the world is taking on a new dimension and when American higher education is expanding overall. Office of Education statistics indicate a rise in college enrollment of from 7.4 million students in 1969 to 10.7 million by 1977 and 11.5 million by 1980. Just to keep its present place in higher education, the field will need to expand by one-third in the next nine years.

Chinese studies have not caught up with less demanding fields. During the period when 412 students earned doctorates in Chinese, 610 doctorates were awarded in Soviet and Eastern European studies by NDEA centers alone, 1,299 in Latin American studies, and 435 in South and Southeast Asian studies.

Overseas Training Facilities

Two overseas facilities have played a vital role in improving the training of students during the past few years. Because mainland China was inaccessible, one was established in Taiwan, the other in Hong Kong.

The Inter-University Program for Chinese Language Studies in Taipei was established in 1963, through the merger of two earlier programs, to provide advanced training in language, written and spoken, to students with two years of college-level Chinese, or its functional equivalent. A total of 295 students, all but ten Americans, have attended the Inter-University Program, which is run by a board representing a consortium of ten (formerly nine) major universities. Since its establishment, this program has accommodated on the campus of National Taiwan University more than half of the American doctoral candidates undertaking advanced training in language institutes in Chinese settings in Asia. Others have gone to Hong Kong, a very few to Singapore, and a number to other language institutes on Taiwan. The chief justification for the Inter-University Program is that it is run by and for the American academic community and thus articulates better than other institutional programs with the previous training and career patterns of American graduate students. (Past support has come from grants by the Carnegie, Ford, and Luce foundations, totaling $803,000 for the period 1963 to June, 1971, or about $100,000 a year.) At present, it claims, rightly in the opinion of many observers, to be the most effective institution open to graduate students for intensive field study of Chinese. It has high standards, is restrictive, and is more costly than other institutes of its kind in Taiwan. The program provides supplementary fellowships to enable more students to use its facilities. Also, it enjoys special dispensation to use Communist materials for those preparing to work on contemporary problems. It therefore can compete in this respect with institutions in Hong Kong but at the same time operate in the only environment where Mandarin Chinese is the standard spoken form of the language, as in mainland China.

Two questions have been raised. Can other institutions adequately serve the needs of American and other graduate students? Excellent as this rather high-cost and competitive facility is by virtue of its location and its special standards and purposes, it serves a relatively small clientele. Not all American graduate students, and almost no non-Americans, use it.

Also established in 1963, the Universities Service Centre (USC) facilitates the research of students, scholars, and other specialists. Incorporated in Hong Kong, and until recently administered by Education and World Affairs under the direction of an international advisory committee chaired by Sir William Hayter, the Centre has been used by 274 scholars in the past seven years, about half of them predoctoral students doing research for their dissertations. (Of 250 who used the Centre up to March 15, 1970, 109 were American and 17 non-American graduate students. With the 24 current users added, the total comes to 140—about 120 American and 20 non-American.) The American graduate students who have used the Centre represent the bulk of those whose dissertations deal with contemporary China.

As long as free access to the mainland is prohibited, Hong Kong remains indispensable for training, orientation, and research. The justification for the Centre is essentially two-fold. First of all, it enables students to make much more efficient use of their time and Hong Kong's resources. Second, special political factors in Hong Kong, the unwillingness of the government to permit substantial numbers of students and scholars without local sponsorship to enter the colony, and the lack of university facilities to sponsor them made it necessary to create a special facility. By March 15, 1970, students and scholars from sixteen countries had used the Centre—about two-thirds of them from the United States. The proportion from other countries has been steadily growing.

Because of the peculiar difficulties facing students and research specialists concerned with contemporary China, training and research costs are high. Students and senior research scholars pay only nominal fees to use the Centre's facilities, the principal costs being carried by foundation grants. When the Centre was established, the advisory committee decided that it would be impossible to charge fees high enough to cover a significant part of costs. To the degree that the Centre accommodated to local conditions and requirements, it did not represent the kind of service whose costs usually are laid upon students and scholars. Charging for the Centre's facilitative services, such as access to the resources of the Union Research Institute and initial provision of working space for twenty scholars, raised other questions. Current fellowship award programs did not cover fees for this type of service. Because the Centre was not properly an educational facility, it did not qualify for tuition payments. Under the circumstances, the Centre could only exist as an international facility; any differentiation among users from different countries seemed unwise.

Students and senior scholars alike appear to be in emphatic agreement that the Centre serves essential purposes. There have been questions, however, about how its facilities can best serve training and orientation. A new director, the former head of the research department of the British Foreign Office and a scholar of nineteenth-century China, has recently been appointed. With time and support, he may be expected to extend and refashion some of the Centre's operations. Clearly the Centre must survive at least until a substitute is devised.

The demise of the Centre would sharply set back the study of contemporary China. Some senior scholars would no doubt find ways to use Hong Kong resources, but students would be hard hit. Russian and Soviet studies needed special facilities for training and research in Yugoslavia and Finland when the Soviet Union was closed; Hong Kong is even more important for contemporary China studies.

V. Research

Despite progress in Chinese studies since World War II, the field is appallingly backward. It still lacks many of the basic research tools that are taken for granted in more developed fields, such as dictionaries, atlases, bibliographies, indices, catalogues of library and research materials, and digests. The field has also suffered from a shortage of research specialists in many branches. In the humanities the following areas need encouragement: art and art history; the history of various key periods and key institutions in the development of Chinese society; literature as a separate field of inquiry; philosophy and the history of ideas.

In the social sciences, virtually all disciplines need further development, and some outside the normal range of language and area studies need to make a start. This is especially true of certain scientific and professional fields. As the number of graduate students and young scholars increases, adequate provision and new opportunities for making full use of their talents become urgent.

Because the number of places with research collections and libraries and other facilities for advanced work is very limited everywhere, efficient use of existing centers is essential.

Research Materials and Collections

There is still great need for better libraries and more trained library personnel. Teaching and reference collections are needed at institutions embarking on Chinese studies. This means acquisition programs, the creation of more and better paid positions, and the training of library personnel. Whether this task can be managed, with current budgets and with current priorities favoring domestic rather than international fields of study and research, is increasingly uncertain. Very few foundation grants of the last fifteen years have adequately supported libraries, whose high-cost operations place an increasing burden on the universities.

Cooperative arrangements for materials acquisition now make it possible to build new libraries and improve the established ones more readily. Cooperative cataloguing and other arrangements long proposed by librarians and scholars to forward the control of Chinese materials still need to be pursued.

Thirteen libraries in North America (one is in Canada) have about 100,000 or more Chinese books. Certain collections are stronger in some fields than others: the Hoover Institution at Stanford, for example, emphasizes the modern and contemporary period; Princeton and Chicago are especially strong on certain aspects of the traditional period. Of these libraries, six have more than 150,000 volumes. Each major library takes many years and millions of dollars to build. None can be duplicated and each should be strengthened, expanded, and efficiently used as an important national resource for work on China. All have expanded their holdings in the past few years. The leading research libraries with their holdings (as of January 1, 1969) are listed in Table II.

Altogether, at the beginning of 1969, the United States

TABLE II
LEADING RESEARCH LIBRARIES AND THEIR HOLDINGS

Name of Library	Number of Volumes in Chinese	Total East Asian Collection (Chinese, Japanese, Korean, Tibetan, Mongolian, Manchu)
Library of Congress	368,081	891,625
Harvard	296,185	429,209
Princeton	175,737	209,478
Chicago	166,308	212,579
Columbia	164,691	274,465
California, Berkeley	150,000 [a]	290,000 [a]
California, L.A.[b]	142,230	192,907
Cornell	133,592	148,764
Yale	107,579	163,822
British Columbia	101,389	124,872
Hoover (Stanford)	99,556	145,551
Washington, Seattle	98,636	132,328
Michigan, Ann Arbor	97,109	195,351

[a] Estimates.

[b] Including 80,000 volumes from the Monumenta Serica Collection.

and Canada had sixty-two libraries and institutional collections of Chinese books—forty-six of them at colleges and universities—with a total of 3,026,729 volumes. The cost of maintaining these libraries in 1968–69 came to about $2.5 million in book purchases and staff salaries.*

The prospects for meeting the needs for research materials have been greatly improved through the establishment of the two facilities mentioned earlier, one in Taiwan, the other in Washington, and through the leadership of the Committee on East Asian Libraries of the Association for Asian Studies. Increasing international cooperation is also significantly improving library acquisitions and control of materials in the United States and elsewhere.

* This figure is derived by dividing the aggregate $4,547,000 budget for East Asian libraries, totaling 4,835,359 volumes, by the proportion of Chinese volumes. See the AAS Committee on Chinese Libraries, *Newsletter,* Association for Asian Studies, No. 29, May 15, 1969, pp. 2, 9.

The Chinese Materials and Research Aids Service Center in Taiwan, sponsored by the Association for Asian Studies, with minimal external support ($47,500), has filled a critical world-wide need. By the end of 1969, five and a half years after it was founded, it had sold almost 600,000 copies—twice the number in the Harvard-Yenching Library —of commissioned reprints of unavailable classics and other publications and of recent Taiwan publications to libraries and scholars in thirty-six countries. Reprints are in special demand by newly developing libraries. Several teaching and reference libraries as well as a few larger libraries, such as those in Canberra, have been able to build strong collections rapidly because of the services of the Taipei facility. In addition to this notable service, the center also produces research aids such as indices, catalogues, directories, and dictionaries.

Similar to the Taiwan center is the <u>Center for Chinese Research Materials in Washington</u>. Sponsored by the Association of Research Libraries, it was established with a substantial grant from the Ford Foundation to facilitate procurement and use of published materials dealing with the Republican and post-1949 periods. One of its aims has been to make widely available research materials on Communist China released by government agencies or obtained in single copies from other sources. It has undertaken the difficult task of trying to stitch together into complete series issues of journals and newspapers scattered throughout the world.

Thanks to these two organizations and a growing number of enterprising librarians and bibliographers cooperating with each other and with government and specialized research institutes, a good deal of progress has been made in expanding scholarly research resources. The available documentation on the Red Guards and the Cultural Revolution is now located at several research centers; essential assistance has been given to new teaching and reference libraries at scores of institutions; classical and modern materials have been reprinted; exchanges have been accelerated; costs have been reduced; and librarians and libraries around the world have been energized. China's failure to order its own research resources, past and present, and make them available has spurred individuals and groups outside of China to extra effort.

Research and Scholarly Aids

There is no good up-to-date general Chinese-English dictionary. (The Mathews dictionary still in common use was published in 1931 for the China Inland Mission and is completely outdated and inadequate.) A new dictionary is of highest priority, as it is needed by all advanced students and scholars in the field. It will be a major and expensive undertaking, but costs might be reduced by using Japanese work as a basis. Japan has a superb Japanese-Chinese general dictionary, but few students and specialists on China have sufficient command of Japanese to take advantage of it.

Specialized dictionaries and reference works—such as dictionaries completed or in preparation in mathematics and law, and the biographical dictionaries of Republican and Communist leaders now appearing—are also needed for Imperial China. The ten-year Ming Biographical History Project, started in 1962 at Columbia University, will meet part of this need when it publishes its indices, guides, and the biographies of about 600 leaders of the Ming dynasty (1368–1644). This project, with a direct investment of more than $350,000 and the participation of some 100 scholars, is a notable example of university and international Sinological cooperation.

Bibliographies and indices are needed to cope with an

impending crisis like that facing many other fields. Materials for the traditional period are still approached through an outdated French compilation. The first general bibliography of works in half a dozen languages on Communist China, begun in 1963, has yet to be published. The Subcommittee on Research on Chinese Society of the Joint Committee on Contemporary China has—at the last possible moment before the deluge of new materials would make the task unmanageable—undertaken to prepare with the use of computers a comprehensive three-volume bibliography on Chinese society. The first volume is scheduled to appear soon. It will cover materials in all major languages on the late traditional to contemporary periods.

Indices are urgently needed for many major bodies of research materials. The Taiwan Chinese Materials and Research Aids Service Center has begun to produce one or two indices of traditional works. With more support, it is ready to expand this work. So far as the contemporary period is concerned, unsuccessful attempts have been made for eight years to find funds to index the Chinese materials translated by U.S. Government agencies, particularly those produced by the United States Joint Publications Research Service (JPRS). A national data bank and reference service is also needed.

Digests and summaries of current materials on China, patterned after the *Current Digest of the Soviet Press,* would make it possible to present intelligibly the information coming out of China. Support for this enterprise has been sought by leading U.S. scholars for about twenty years without success.

While this review of research tools points up the underdeveloped state of Chinese studies, it has also revealed movement in every area. Projects cited above will open vast realms of materials and data to social scientists, historians, and others for more penetrating studies of Chinese society in most major areas, classical and modern.

Should scholars on the mainland and in Taiwan turn more energetically to scholarship and prepare requisite scholarly tools, the pressures elsewhere to develop aids to research and study would be greatly diminished. Furthermore, the Japanese, as they develop their work on China, will lighten the burden of scholars in America and Europe. The Chinese Linguistics Project at Princeton University, as well as a number of other language research projects, many undertaken by NDEA centers, might also contribute to the preparation of a dictionary and other tools of research. The whole enterprise needs strong support and the leadership of one or two dedicated scholars.

Research Facilities

Most scholarly research in this country has been undertaken at major university centers. Brought together in an academic setting are senior scholars and specialists, major collections of research materials, a body of graduate students to provide recruits for the field and to serve as part-time or summer research assistants, supporting administrative services within a stable institutional framework, and the like. Teachers at these institutions can engage in part-time research. Full-time research specialists, those on research leave, and scholars from institutions with inadequate resources have found such an environment stimulating for productive work.

At these university centers people collaborate on such enterprises as linguistic projects and the preparation of biographical references; joint research programs with non-area specialists on subjects like Chinese education, science, or personality; long-term projects on arms control or economic and social development.

Major centers of Chinese studies at large universities (with budgets from $250,000 to $325,000, excluding the costs of library and major projects) have provided facilities and substantial support for ten to twelve full-time researchers and the part-time and summer research of seven or eight faculty members. They have also paid for some research assistance, provided modest funds for conferences and for travel and field research in Asia, covered costs of editorial work and publication subsidies, and maintained supporting services. Some centers have also undertaken contract research, with its special requirements. At the lower end of the scale, small centers with three or four research specialists and without special supporting editorial or publishing and operational services have operated on budgets varying from $25,000 to $60,000.

A few government-related or -sponsored research facilities, notably the RAND Corporation, the Institute of Defense Analyses (IDA), and the Research Analysis Corporation, have over the past ten years enlisted perhaps thirty or forty scholars for significant periods of time and have supported their work. Very few scholars have entered full-time government service for research. Even now, there are fewer than half a dozen specialists with doctorates in the Chinese field employed by the U.S. Government. This contrasts with the Soviet and Eastern European field, where according to one estimate 75 to 100 Ph.D.'s work for the government. This contrast reflects, in part the fact that the Chinese field has still not produced enough scholars in the social sciences to fulfill the faculty needs of universities.

Research Grants

Most of the postdoctoral research on China has been supported by university funds, the research funds awarded by committees of the American Council of Learned Societies and the Social Science Research Council, and other special-project funds. In addition to the Ming Biographical

History Project and the Chinese Society Bibliography Project mentioned above, the Committee on Chinese Thought of the Association for Asian Studies and various subcommittees of the ACLS and SSRC have sponsored research conferences that have also supported some research.

The Joint Committee on Asian Studies has given major support to postdoctoral research, primarily relating to Imperial China. In the years 1959–71, it has made 72 research awards, totaling $321,163. Of these, 32 have been for work in history, 13 in language and literature, and 8 in art and archaeology.

For modern and contemporary China (1900 to the present), the major source of postdoctoral research funds has been the Joint Committee on Contemporary China. In ten years, 1961–70, 136 research awards, totaling $860,815, have been made to 119 scholars from 68 institutions. Forty-seven awards have been for work in history, 28 in political science, 12 in economics, 11 in law, 10 in sociology, and a few distributed through several other disciplines. One partial listing presents titles of more than 165 publications resulting from these awards up to 1969. A substantial proportion of the work done on post-1949 China has been carried out at the Universities Service Centre in Hong Kong, much of it based upon interviews with Chinese from the mainland.

In the past few years, the research of American scholars and senior graduate students, buttressed by significant contributions from scholars in Europe, has produced a major change in our knowledge of China and our scholarly approach. Although our grasp of our own Western heritage and modern Western societies is still far ahead, we now have moved to a point where we can contemplate and study China, past and present, in "professional" and serious ways that go beyond the purposeful limits of missionary, business, and diplomatic needs.

VI. The Financing of Chinese Studies

Higher education in America has grown rapidly since World War II, especially since the mid-1950's. In the academic year 1955–56, 2.8 million students were enrolled in colleges and universities whose expenditures totaled $4.1 billion. By 1968–69 the number of students had risen to 7.4 million and expenditures to $20.4 billion.

It should be noted that the private sector of higher education has lagged far behind the public sector in growth in enrollment and budgets.* Yet, it is in the private universities that the main resources for training and research on China exist. Many factors are responsible. These colleges and universities have enjoyed greater opportunity, free as they are from surveillance and control by state legislatures, to pioneer in nonutilitarian humanistic and social science studies. Because of their original classical, religious, and missionary orientations, some of these institutions had developed faculty and library resources relating to non-Western civilizations fairly early. Most state institutions, on the other hand, felt Asian affairs to be more of

* See Howard R. Bowen, "Financial Needs of the Campus," in Robert H. Connery, *The Corporation and the Campus,* Proceedings of the Academy of Political Science, XXX, 1 (1970), pp. 75–93.

a national than a regional concern, and thus not their responsibility. The contrast lessened as time went on, even before World War II. Now in Washington, California, New York, Michigan, Illinois, and Indiana, and less markedly in many other states, attitudes have changed. However, at the time when the development effort in Chinese studies was undertaken, private not state institutions (with a few exceptions) had the resources needed to support professional standards of training, especially for graduate work.

Because none of the colleges and universities possessed sufficient funds for major new programs to expand the study of China, a large infusion of external support, primarily for graduate training, was essential. These funds were, however, significantly supplemented and, in some programs, more than matched by the universities once given the opportunity for expansion.

The major outlay of funds took place in the period 1958–59 to 1970 when more than $40 million of foundation and government funds was invested in academic instruction, materials, research, and facilities to promote the study and understanding of China. The main sources of funds for Chinese studies from 1933 to the present are indicated in Table III.

These figures make clear that the Ford Foundation provided the basic resources needed to develop and expand the field. (See Appendix V for a list of Ford Foundation grants.) From the beginning, it expected the federal government to finance some essential parts of the program, but its trustees were prepared in any case to meet needs that they felt were as critical for the country as the development of Soviet studies had been a decade and a half earlier. Because of their essential role in shaping the field, it is useful to examine further the grants made by the Ford Foundation. Its annual commitment of funds varied from year to year as the field developed, the major outlays

TABLE III
EXTERNAL FUNDS FOR CHINESE STUDIES IN INSTITUTIONS OF
HIGHER EDUCATION IN THE UNITED STATES

Foundation	1933–45	1946–57	1958/59–70	Total
Rockefeller Foundation	$741,047	$ 492,439	$ 278,261	$ 1,511,747
Carnegie Corporation			1,739,000	1,739,000
Ford Foundation		2,986,009	$23,821.201	$26,807,210
Rockefeller Brothers Fund			50,000	50,000
Henry Luce Foundation			45,000	45,000
Total Foundations	741,047	3,478,448	25,933,462	30,152,957
NDEA Centers			4,800,000	4,800,000
NDFL Fellowships			8,950,000	8,950,000
NSF			250,000	250,000
National Humanities Foundation			40,000	40,000
Other			1,000,000	1,000,000
Total U.S. Government			$15,040,000	$15,040,000
Totals	$741,047	$3,478,448	$40,973,462	$45,192,957

TABLE IV
FORD FOUNDATION GRANTS IN SUPPORT OF THE STUDY
AND UNDERSTANDING OF CHINA, 1952–69
(millions of dollars, rounded)

	Grants in U.S. (Including $107,000 a Year Averaged for FAFP)	Grants Abroad	Totals
1952–58	$3.127	.030	3.157
1959	.126	.100	.226
1960	3.023	—	3.023
1961	4.452	.020	4.472
1962	3.267	.401	3.668
1963	1.371	.130	1.501
1964	.492	.553	1.045
1965	1.757	—	1.757
1966	1.642	.018	1.660
1967	6.560	1.063	7.623
1968	.699	.465	1.164
1969	.432	.020	.452
Actual Totals	$26,947,710	$2,800,000	$29,747,710

being in the years 1960–62 and 1967, as indicated in Table IV.

Besides the other major contributions, fellowship support came from the National Defense Education Act and from universities prepared to put up matching funds to create NDEA centers. These sources added another $10 million to support instruction in language and culture that would not otherwise have been available in regular university budgets.

Other foundations and agencies had important supporting roles. The Carnegie Corporation, for example, provided funds totaling $1,739,000 for several special enterprises. These included supplying research resources for the study of Chinese society, establishing the Universities Service Centre in Hong Kong, teaching Chinese in secondary schools, and training journalists for work in East Asia. The Rockefeller Foundation, after the war, shifted most of its funds in the China field to supporting work outside the United States. It had a special interest, however, in developing Chinese legal studies and work on Tibet within the United States. Of the $650,800 it granted for work on China in 1958–69, $279,000 was spent in the United States, a substantial part being for the special purposes mentioned.

As noted above, because of the critical need for more trained scholars, the Ford Foundation decided to assist universities already possessing basic resources that would require the least additional investment to develop and expand training and research on modern and contemporary China, especially in the social sciences. The largest institutional grants were made to the four, later six, centers where substantial multidisciplinary programs were emerging, with lesser grants to other institutions for supporting or specialized studies. It also made substantial funds available to national bodies for fellowship and research programs. The main American recipients in the period 1959–69 were:

Harvard University	$2,913,000
Social Science Research Council	2,745,000
University of Michigan	2,525,000
Columbia University	2,039,000
University of California (Berkeley)	1,800,000
University of Washington	1,742,000
Cornell University	1,363,260
Foreign Area Fellowship Program (Administered by ACLS)	1,177,745
Stanford University	1,503,000
American Council of Learned Societies	641,800
Princeton University	580,000
Yale University	375,000

In addition, from 1958 to 1969, the Ford Foundation has made grants of almost $3 million to support study of

TABLE V

FORD AND ROCKEFELLER GRANTS TO SELECTED COUNTRIES
IN SUPPORT OF CHINESE STUDIES, 1958–59 TO 1970

Countries	Rockefeller Grants	Ford Grants	Totals
United Kingdom	$ 66,275	$ 740,000	$ 806,275
India		536,000	536,000
Republic of China: Taiwan	86,800	421,000	507,800
Germany	29,600	325,000	354,600
Japan	83,525	253,000	336,525
International associations		150,000	150,000
Korea		143,000	143,000
Australia		125,000	125,000
Canada		97,000	97,000
France	34,250		34,250
The Netherlands	30,000		30,000
Hong Kong	15,000	10,000	25,000
Denmark	15,625		15,625
Italy	5,000		5,000
Total	$366,075	$2,800,000	$3,166,075

China in other countries. The Rockefeller Foundation also has assisted many of the same countries and institutions. Table V summarizes the principal grants by these two foundations to other countries for work relating to China.

In Great Britain and India, some of these funds helped to establish new programs or institutions. Most of the grants, however, were made to strengthen existing programs or projects. In a few cases, these grants, offered on a matching or conditional basis, succeeded in mobilizing additional local funds for the support of Chinese studies.

Foundation and government funds and the university funds channeled into Chinese studies have supported a wide range of activities. In general terms, the external funds available in 1958–70 have been used for the following purposes:

Training Fellowships	$12,000,000
University Centers and Programs (Instruction, Research, Facilities, Fellowships)	20,000,000
National Research and Development Programs	5,000,000
Special Facilities (for materials, overseas language training, etc.)	2,000,000
Miscellaneous	1,000,000
Total	$40,000,000

Part of the funds granted to universities have been used to build faculty strength. Practices vary a great deal. On the basis of "soft money" or grants from foundations, some institutions, like Columbia, have made tenure commitments if sufficient funds to cover ten years of salary were available. Some state universities and smaller liberal-arts colleges have used these funds to recruit short-term faculty members who have then been transferred to regular departmental budgets once courses proved successful. Others, like Harvard, have insisted on fully financed endowed chairs before making tenure appointments. Private universities, dependent as they are on gift and endowment funds, clearly have larger needs for external funds to ensure the recruitment of permanent faculty.

Unless endowment funds continue to grow, private universities, despite library and research resources that are not duplicable without extravagant cost, are likely to fall behind the expanding public universities as Chinese studies develop. In terms of cost and rational use of resources, there are strong arguments that may be even more compelling in the years immediately ahead to utilize the resources of a dozen leading centers (all but three of them private) as national centers supported in considerable measure by local, state, federal, and foundation funds. This is especially applicable to graduate education and research.

As private gifts, federal funds, and foundation support have declined, a substantial (but unrecorded) number of faculty members engaged in teaching courses and developing programs relating to China have been placed on regular departmental budgets. In this respect, the effort to integrate China and non-Western studies into our educational system has been partly successful. However, the conclusion of some twenty scholars who participated in the Conference on the Status of Studies of Modern and Contemporary China held in March, 1968, still remains true for the field as a whole: "There is not one of the centers in the universities that possesses a full complement of faculty members covering all the basic disciplines that a fully integrated center should enjoy."*

* JCCC, ACLS/SSRC, "Conference Report, the Status of Studies of Modern and Contemporary China," New York, March 15–16, 1968.

In the course of normal growth, these additions might be anticipated. But present conditions put constraints on the training received by the present generation of graduate students: Some 400 to 500 of them (half the enrollment) probably merit and will get doctoral degrees. These emerging scholars, together with the 400 who have completed their work since 1960, will set the standards for the field and the country for several decades to come.

One point seems clear at present: The leading centers will and should hold their lead for at least the next decade. If they are allowed to decline, grave gaps and a setback of standards will result. The rapidly expanding state university systems now entering the field will not for some time be able to match international standards for either advanced training or research.

Another financial question relates to the education of the present generation of students, both graduate and undergraduate, committed to Chinese studies. Even with an attrition rate of 50 per cent among graduate students now enrolled, there remain some 400 to 500 students and another 50 to 60 undergraduate applicants a year who by all present academic criteria merit advanced training. NDFL fellowship support for all foreign areas was cut from about $5.5 million in 1968–70 to $3.27 million in 1971, and fellowships from 1,188 to 750. The allotment of 90 to 100 fellowships for study of China will not meet the minimal requirements for the best of the present students. Should this program be resuscitated, the situation will be eased. Nonetheless, there still remains the question, which is discussed elsewhere, of funds for improving standards.

One aspect of the field has gone unnoted. About 40 per cent of the doctorates granted in Chinese studies in the decade of development have been to native speakers of Chinese, virtually all from Taiwan and Hong Kong. The major cost of training these scholars, about 145 in number, has been borne by universities and university centers. All together, their training has meant an investment of perhaps $2 to $2.5 million. Should fellowship and study-work funds be drastically reduced, such students now in training, numbering perhaps 200 or more, would be resourceless.

VII. State of the Field: Problems and Prospects

When the "developmental decade" began in 1958–59, contemporary expectations and conditions affected the approach of scholars and institutions seeking to improve American resources for understanding China. There were, for example, expectations that published information and scholarly output from the People's Republic of China would continue to expand and would improve in quality and that scholarly communications and access to China would generally and steadily increase for everyone, including Americans. Both expectations proved false. During the decade, Chinese scholarly activities suffered severe setbacks. More than 500 scholarly and professional journals ceased publication, access to China became increasingly restricted, and China became more isolated.

The nature of the Sino-Soviet alliance, although already observably uneasy, suggested that the study of contemporary China might fruitfully borrow from the development of Soviet studies. In the cold-war setting of that time, the universities already possessing resources for both Chinese and Soviet studies were thought to be in the best position to take the lead in understanding the Chinese face of Communism and in training new scholars and specialists on

China. Augmenting and supporting the training programs which each university assumed the responsibility to develop within its own framework, it was expected that research, planning, and the development of special resources would be provided by the Joint Committee on Contemporary China. As mentioned earlier, this committee was modeled upon the Joint Committee on Slavic Studies, which had just published a three-volume review of more than a decade of intensive development. This review recorded significant achievements: the production of a large number of research monographs and studies, disciplinary and institutional growth, diffusion of courses and knowledge in the curricula of secondary schools and colleges, the training in about a decade of 100 specialists with doctorates, and about 500 others with master's degrees.

During the next decade, developments in China and American relations with China, contrary to expectations, not only produced special problems for training and research, but also influenced recruitment and training of students. Moreover, the difficulties of reorienting the American public and educational system to take full account of non-Western civilizations were not fully appreciated. After successful efforts to persuade Congress that the American approach to non-Western countries should go beyond the goals of the National Defense Education Act of 1958 to those incorporated in the International Education Act of 1966, the vision embodied in that Act was not pursued. Possibly it has been abandoned for this generation.

Pace and Patterns of Growth

How might the developmental activities during this decade of academic and scholarly effort in Chinese studies be assessed? First, the approach was far more decentralized than in the development of Soviet studies, where prior to 1958 new outside resources were concentrated in fewer institutions. This was partly the result of the way in which the implementation of the NDEA affected training patterns and use of existing university resources. Federal funds for East Asian studies, as for all other non-Western and critical area studies, were much more broadly dispensed than were the foundation grants which earlier had been the principal means for developing work on the Soviet Union.

The allocation of supplementary foundation funds, in turn, was influenced in part by this pattern, which, indeed, seemed reasonable given the distribution of university resources. This dispersion of support, however, meant weak coordination for monitoring and controlling standards in the training of both graduate and undergraduate students. Prevailing degree requirements were modified on an individual university basis to accommodate the additional requirements for those working on non-Western areas within the disciplines rather than in area departments. As a consequence of the creation of NDEA centers within the universities to handle funds allocated by the Act, language training (supported primarily by NDEA funds) tended to be separated from research and work in the social sciences that depended upon foundation funds.

This partly accounts for the fact that in Chinese studies the area programs that were strong have remained strong —history and language and literature—and that the social sciences, with the exception of political science, have not made notable progress. Moreover, some of the social-science disciplines have been hard for Chinese studies to penetrate and not only because of their anti-regional and often pro-Western orientations. Another reason was the American emphasis on field research in a number of disciplines which made an inaccessible area like China, when the Soviet Union was becoming more accessible, even less attractive as a specialization. Hence, sociology, economics, anthropology, geography, and cognate fields did not respond quickly to the challenges of finding new long-distance methods of training and research to deal with China. Even specialists in international affairs and security problems tended to neglect China as a subject of serious concern, as have specialists working within the context of science policy and economic development.

So far as training is concerned, some fields remain weak, others altogether neglected; standards in the social sciences still leave much to be desired. This will probably remain true so long as the study of China and other non-Western areas presents special problems and is viewed, as is often the case, as adding only marginal knowledge. Put in a somewhat different way, proponents of extending Chinese studies into new disciplines have accommodated themselves to established procedures to win acceptance and support. A modest "intruder" has tailored itself to the standards and perspectives of the large enterprises where it seeks inclusion and legitimacy.

The strategy of development had a further weakness. The various committees, especially the Joint Committee on Contemporary China and the Committee on Chinese Civilization, were concerned with research and related problems, not with training. Moreover, the two committees did not coordinate their work in any real sense, partly because the JCCC started with a Soviet model before it. To divide training and research may be functionally efficient in well-established fields of study, but it has not contributed to the coherent and balanced development of Chinese studies. Furthermore, the Gould House Conference of 1959 was the only meeting that took a broad look at the field until 1968 when the JCCC sponsored a review conference, but both of these gatherings confined themselves to post-1949 China. In Russian studies there was, on the other hand, a comprehensive evaluation of all aspects of the field in 1957–58, and in Japanese studies a similar appraisal was made in 1969–70. Because no complex and broad scholarly field such as Chinese studies can move forward without a reasonable consensus among its institutional, disciplinary, and scholarly leaders, the field would benefit from factual analysis, airing, and discussion—both as to present problems and future direction. The pressing issues include the place of non-Western studies in American education, the role and function of the study of China in the United States, the organization of the field, and the relation between the study of traditional and contemporary China.

Divisions

The organization of the field has raised a number of questions. The division between "traditionalists" and "modernists" has been the subject of considerable comment. This same division apparently affects other countries. It is not merely a product of America's domestic conditions. It probably reflects in part, the sharp break between the traditionalists and modernists in China, where a century of controversy colors the attitudes of intellectuals and scholars and has, in some ways, been intensified during the past two decades of Communist rule.

In Mao's China, the past is explicitly rejected. Campaigns are mounted to destroy the "four bads" of the past because the past seems to fetter China's future. Scholarly study of traditional culture has atrophied; much of what remains is a branch of propaganda, serving to reorient minds and reinforce the values of something entirely new. The historian sees the past in the present; the creators of the future often see little in the past beyond something to escape or exploit.

All of these elements contribute to controversy, uncertainty, and tension among outsiders interested in China. Is the study and understanding of China to be a Sinological venture into the past of a great civilization, or is it to be an understanding and preparation for work with China's present leaders and people? Do we come to postrevolutionary China after studying its past, or are we attuning ourselves to their present, however leached of past riches?

Our academic institutions have rightly nurtured a predilection for the past, and for many reasons. Under existing conditions, China's past, ironically, is in many ways more accessible to us than its present. Contemporary Chinese realities and experience are not only uncomfortable and provocative but remain abstract and of little utility for us since we do not have working relations with the vast population of mainland Chinese. On the other hand, China's past is fascinating and in its legacies perhaps more temptingly rich than historic Egypt, Greece, and Rome, if not as relevant to us. The effort to understand the present runs into problems. We look at China—apart from international politics—more through its past than its present. Illusions and myths thus abound. In the meantime, however, we have fostered wide-ranging interest in China, both past and present, in order to think of China in multidimensional terms. The result is organizationally untidy, but intellectually enriching.

The strong and painful divisions that marked the postwar McCarthy era were successfully transcended so far as they affected institutional and scholarly cooperation. Broadening the field at the end of the 1950's depended upon bringing together some of the established academic leaders in the field with people of different orientations. This was achieved by making the ACLS and SSRC responsible for new task-oriented committees. Had the Association for Asian Studies, for example, been asked to broaden the field, some observers feel that established scholars at the major universities, nearly all focused on traditional China, would have prolonged Chinese studies as an isolated specialized enterprise within the academic system. It would seem then that until those working on contemporary and Imperial China develop a broader consensus, it would probably do more harm than good to force centralization on the field through grant-making and other activities.

The Joint Committee on Contemporary China has been a carefully balanced body, its members representing the major regions of the country, the major university centers, a variety of disciplines, and individuals who are committed to working with colleagues cooperatively within the committee framework. On the whole, this approach seemed to succeed. Divisions were increasingly overcome and new orientations accepted.

Critics of the JCCC charge, however, that smaller institutions were not represented, nor were younger scholars until 1965. With able and well-trained younger scholars moving into a good many institutions, broader age and institutional representation is now possible. The complaints recorded from some students and scholars, however, tend to stress political bias and conservatism. The Committee is charged with subservience to foundations and the U.S. Government and with a failure to actively foster measures and studies that might have changed U.S. policies on China and Asia.

This is difficult ground to cover without agreement on the nature of the academic enterprise. There are former government officers who are prepared to testify that the views of China scholars, written and spoken, have had a major role in shifting official views toward a new way of looking at the China problem. Many of the so-called establishment scholars have urged changes in American policy. The real test of the success of Chinese studies, some have implied, should be its impact on government policy. This contention, however, raises questions not only for scholars working on China, but for the entire academic and scholarly community. Specialists on China, after all, represent a minute proportion of the university community of scholars.

The Erosion of Resources

In many basic fields, Chinese scholarship, both in the People's Republic of China and on Taiwan, has eroded or even disappeared. During the last decade on the Chinese mainland, as already noted, more than 500 scholarly journals have ceased publication, academic and research institutions have been dismantled, senior scholars left in a limbo of uncertainty and inactivity, and the serious training of new scholars is still not evident. The full impact affects those areas of central concern to social scientists. The natural sciences and technologies have been less seriously affected.

Moreover, the study of contemporary developments on the China mainland is restricted to special government agencies and completely undeveloped in academic institutions. China's energetic and often brilliant group of pre-war historians and social scientists, who sought to understand and reinterpret its past and present, are vanishing and not being replaced. On Taiwan, the Government of the Republic of China has also given priority to the scientific and technological fields as they relate to economic development and military strength, and has neglected the study of Chinese tradition and culture.

China is becoming an intellectual and cultural steppe-land. What this means for those seeking to understand China is dismayingly plain. Outsiders barred from China cannot possibly do what China's own scholars should be doing—studying, analyzing, and interpreting China's present developments from all possible perspectives. For every other major country, foreign scholars base their work primarily on the work of indigenous scholars and analysts. The problem is compounded by continued lack of access to mainland China—thus the difficulty, and, for Americans, impossibility, of exposing new generations of social-science students to the society and country on which they specialize. This difficulty is accentuated, not only by limited Chinese research in the social sciences and the lack of opportunity to develop collaborative research, but also by the paucity or unavailability of publications.

The Role of Chinese Scholars and Students

In the past, native Chinese experts and scholars, indispensable for language instruction and work on traditional China, have had a unique place in raising Chinese studies to a professional scholarly level in this country. Many of them are refugees from China. They belong to a generation that had both Chinese and Western training and experience—scholars and instructors who could work in two worlds. Now the supply of talent from China has dwindled rapidly. Young Chinese on the mainland and in Taiwan are no longer trained in the high standards that once prevailed. In their place is a new group—the Chinese who have received their advanced training in this country.

Questions about the role and influence of foreign-born Chinese scholars take various guises. One observer, commenting on senior and junior American experts on China, says that a third group must be added—"the Chinese expatriates, who would never have been admitted to America if they had not been considered politically respectable— i.e., non-Marxist and anti-Peking."* Older Chinese expatriates should be distinguished from the younger group

* Owen Lattimore, Review of *China in Crisis,* in *Political Science Quarterly,* LXXXV, 2 (June, 1970), 351.

of Chinese scholars recently trained in this country and, in smaller numbers, in Europe. The contribution of the older group is plain, but only the most eminent won teaching posts at major universities, mostly because of such handicaps as weakness in the English language, lack of qualifications to supervise thesis and dissertation research, lack of teaching facility, and also because of their sometimes strong political views and weak bargaining position as refugees. While some of the younger American-trained scholars of Chinese origin suffer from the same handicaps, many have surmounted them.

Other problems arise. Because of the complex and uncertain character of our relations with China, both groups raise questions of a political character, but in differing degree. Some Americans are concerned about the impact that Chinese or Chinese-Americans in centers of Chinese studies may have in shaping American academic relations with Chinese institutions both in the People's Republic and in Taiwan. Many students from Taiwan are either hostile to the Nationalist government or, conversely, suspected of being its agents. Many of those from Hong Kong or of mainland origin are thought to be politically biased against China. For these reasons in part, very few have served on committees devoted either to research or to scholarly relations with Chinese institutions. The Joint Committee on Contemporary China, for example, has never had a member of Chinese origin, fearing either possible embarrassment to the scholar or unnecessary complications in dealing with official agencies in Taiwan, mainland China, or elsewhere.

As noted earlier, about 40 per cent, or 145, of the doctorates in the China field in the last decade were awarded to native speakers of Chinese, primarily from Taiwan and Hong Kong. Almost all of them came to this country for graduate training and have become or are seeking to become permanent residents or citizens. It is possible that the United States in the past few years has provided more advanced training to Chinese in various fields of Chinese studies than all Chinese universities combined.

Present trends indicate that, during a period when both political and personal issues have high saliency, about one-third of the next generation of academically trained specialists on China in the United States will be of Chinese origin, most of them linked to families and groups in Hong Kong, Taiwan, and the People's Republic.

On the positive side and in the absence of more intensive early training of American-born students interested in China, these immigrant Chinese students will help to ensure scholarly standards, especially in linguistic and documentary competence and cultural orientation.

Standards of Training

Some observers point to the inadequate training of most American and Western scholars and the superficial and abstract quality of much research, particularly on modern and contemporary China. Less than full interpretive use is made of available data. Virtually no American scholars who are not of Chinese origin are bilingual; not more than two or three can write a scholarly article in Chinese for a Chinese publication; less than a handful have been students in a Chinese academic institution working in competition with Chinese students; and few have any sense of ease in a wholly Chinese environment.

If American and foreign scholars working on China can no longer rely on Chinese scholarship, do not have the support of well-trained Chinese scholarly colleagues, and are handicapped by limited access to China, they need equipment and background of a far higher order than they now have. Proportionately more Europeans than Americans are receiving conditioning to supplement their disciplinary skills. Without this, American scholarship will be narrow and technical. To achieve the highest quality, it must take into account cultural nuances and a grasp of the range of Chinese social and historical experience.

The Academic Environment

Another source of apprehension in the United States, as well as among some scholars abroad, is the impact on Chinese studies of current problems plaguing American educational and research institutions. At this stage in its development and facing problems of unique difficulty, the whole effort to develop the requisite scholarly talent and resources for understanding China might, some argue, suffer a setback that would be felt for at least a generation. This fear is understandable considering the abandonment of the goals of the International Education Act of 1966, the shift in educational and public priorities from international to domestic problems, the apparently declining sense of China as a security threat, and the growing propensity to exploit China for domestic political purposes on and off the campus.

Unless these difficulties are properly handled, they may undermine much of the progress recently made.

Measuring Future Needs

Other related questions arise. How do we measure what we want or need in terms of resources? Criteria can vary enormously. Under present circumstances, we may have enough trained scholars to fill university teaching posts currently available. But this raises further questions. Are the number of posts open to China specialists based upon purely parochial trends in our expanding educational system? Can Chinese studies be considered in the larger context of universalizing our educational perspectives and knowledge to provide the same treatment of non-Western cultures that we accord Western civilization? To do so would mean major revisions in our elementary and secondary school systems, the retraining of teachers, and the large-scale rewriting of texts. UNESCO's efforts in this direction have been applauded but practically ignored. The aborting of the International Education Act of 1966 is not reassuring.

Is the measure of our need to be determined by the practical requirements of business, government, and other institutions involved in international affairs? These needs change, in part, with the state of our relations with China. War seems to require numerous specialists for government agencies in many fields, peace fewer. Commercial enterprises require different kinds of specialists, usually in limited numbers.

Within the framework of Oriental studies, the Soviet Union for more than ten years has given priority to China. But its efforts appear to be no more and probably considerably less successful than ours, even taking into account the differences in context and approach. Australia gives higher priority to Japan and Southeast Asia. Much depends upon our perspective and view of our future and China's. Although we cannot see ten years ahead, we must plan now for what we think we shall probably need and want then.

VIII. Conclusions and Recommendations

The foregoing review of Chinese studies in the United States (and to a lesser extent other countries) has led to certain conclusions that can be restated as follows:

First, China continues to be of great interest to many countries and to many diverse groups of people. The kaleidoscopic shift of events within China, its radically experimental social and political movements and programs, and the immense presence of land and people have generated concern, excitement, or curiosity outside of China. Near one end of the spectrum of response is the Soviet Union, which set out in the mid-1960's to develop major research resources relating to China because it appears to see China as a potential threat of massive dimensions. Near the other pole are anti-establishment groups who seek from Maoism or China ideas to nurture their views.

In between is a wide range of groups. Some are concerned about international relations, some see the Chinese experience as relevant to their own problems and those of other peoples, and some view the study of China as an intellectual challenge. Even in countries where China appears a less ominous military threat than it did a few years ago, a growing number of people have become interested in China, especially students. To this extent, it may be easier now than a decade ago to recruit people to learn about China. Although some argue that the contemporary Chinese experience is sterile and that the country's immediate prospects are bleak, on balance, there is convincing evidence that the need to know and understand China will increase, not decline.

Second, there has been marked growth during the past decade in Chinese studies and in the resources needed for training and research. Rapid expansion of postgraduate training has tended to overshadow other areas of development. The number of graduate students in historical and modern-contemporary studies has gone up from 143 in 1951 to about 325 in 1964 to 750 in 1967 and about 1,000 at present. In the modern and contemporary field, there were about 100 graduate students in 1960 (more than half of whom were in post-1800 history), 260 in 1964, and 680 in 1967. Currently, there are about 700 graduate students specializing in the modern-contemporary periods—about 300 in history and 400 in other social sciences—with perhaps 300 more graduate students doing advanced work in traditional history, linguistics, literature, philosophy, art, and archaeology. This rate of development has produced strains and probably some loss in quality. Although hard to document, the stress on graduate rather than undergraduate training may also reflect some of the overall tensions in American education and culture. Undergraduate education makes so many claims on student time that "exotic" and demanding fields, such as Chinese studies, face resistance. However, more than 100 colleges and universities now give Chinese language instruction to over 4,000 undergraduates.

Although research publications have increased markedly, major scholarly publication has been retarded in some disciplines. Senior faculty members have been pre-occupied with tasks other than research. Furthermore, the problems of access and data have been intractable, especially those facing social scientists.

Third, resources for understanding China are still inadequate to meet those goals generally considered of high priority. These include reasonably comprehensive scholarly knowledge of China and the Chinese; incorporation of knowledge and data about China in the major disciplines; deparochializing American education, especially at the college and secondary school levels; diffusion of existing knowledge to the general public; and training specialists for nonacademic careers in a wide range of fields that relate to China or involve the Chinese.

Problems of quality and quantity remain. The pattern of American postgraduate training militates against the kind and length of training many fields require to develop competence and excellence. Note has already been taken of the rare ability among American scholars to write Chinese, and the almost complete lack of American enrollment in Chinese universities. General knowledge of China is often woefully deficient because students concentrate early on their disciplinary specialties. Historians often know little of China's political and economic systems, and social scientists often have little historic perspective. However difficult the language, or the culture, professional mastery of a field—rather than graduate school schedules—should be the controlling criterion for at least some of our ablest young scholars. High qualitative goals will, of course, be in much closer reach for graduate students who received language training, general orientation, and, ideally, a year's undergraduate exposure to a Chinese community.

In other countries, undergraduates receive basic systematic training in Chinese language and history, with

Chinese the primary, sometimes almost exclusive, field of study. Therefore, very little formal training is given to postgraduate students. In the United States until recently, most formal training, including language, was graduate. In some ways, this pattern has improved courses and curriculum, but it has also exacted harsh requirements of the students. The net effect is highly intensive training that makes for narrowness, lack of acculturation to a Chinese setting, and less than genuine mastery of the language. This does not mean, for example, that an economist specialized on China is not reliable in his economic judgments on China. It does mean that he is not generally knowledgeable about China, or equipped as much more than a technician. This illustration can be turned in countless ways.

The quantitative weakness shows up primarily in certain fields. At a minimum, it would seem essential to have sixty economists working on China a decade from now, not twenty as at present. Sociologists and others who are strongly field-research oriented have not been attracted to China because of its inaccessibility. Yet the China mainland is a social laboratory of unique interest even for study at a distance.

The introduction, diffusion, role, and development of modern science and technology in China is almost completely neglected by scholars. Nonetheless, it is clearly impossible to have a balanced knowledge of China's rapid development without understanding how it is putting modern science and technology to use. There are similar gaps of knowledge in medicine and social welfare.

Fourth, Chinese studies, like other fields, faces a current crisis. The opening of new posts for graduates has been sharply reduced for a number of reasons. The allocation of public and private funds is shifting from international to domestic concerns. Economic constraints—inflation and recession—have slowed educational expansion. A current of anti-intellectualism combined with a desire to retract international involvements has led to a further drop in concern with Asia, and the China threat, much overplayed, does not seem to loom as large. Whatever the reasons, the failure of Congress to fund the International Education Act because of the costs of the Vietnam war, and the willingness of the present administration to eliminate special support for foreign language and area-training fellowships and centers, coupled with the budgetary problems of colleges and universities, have created problems that need to be faced directly and responsibly.

With our present resources, we can and should consider new strategies for developing Chinese studies and, at the same time, find new ways in which anticipated needs can be better served.

Fifth, over the past twelve years a large investment of time, effort, and money has been put into developing Chinese studies. The Ford Foundation alone has invested about $30 million, and the U.S. Government and the universities together through the National Defense Education Act have spent a similar amount. Hundreds of students have committed years to preparing themselves for teaching and other careers in the field.

This investment needs to be protected and fully and constructively used. The decade of development has created resources that can be productive now and for thirty years ahead if properly used and sustained. If scholars and graduate students are not given appropriate posts, their morale will falter and many will leave the field, at high cost to them and to those who trained them. Outside of China, the United States has the world's largest (if still inadequate) group of graduate students—between 900 and 1,000. At least one-third are working for doctorates and thus basically committed to professional careers as teachers and researchers in the field. Meeting their needs and providing opportunities for work are of primary importance. The other two-thirds provide our society with a further opportunity to bring people with a knowledge of China into public affairs, communications, the professions, business, and a diverse range of national and international activities.

In addition, there are university teaching and research centers, teaching programs, and library and research facilities that need greater support in order to meet criteria for sustained excellence.

Sixth, within the field, new emphases, patterns of support, and procedures need consideration. The general ferment for reordering college and university campuses has also affected people working on China. In addition, there has been widespread uneasiness about American policies toward China. The stirrings of an imitative radical Yellow Power movement among young American Chinese is complicated by the large number of alien Chinese students on our campuses (about 18,000), China's attraction for part of the New Left, and perhaps certain residual effects of earlier dissensions, highlighted during the McCarthy period. All these factors have tended to create a dynamic desire for new directions and more diversity, and have also produced controversy about such matters as the relation of the field to government. Finally, there are questions about the responsibility of those in Chinese studies for developing undergraduate courses and better programs of public education.

*   *   *

The conclusions reached by this study provide a basis for certain recommendations for the future development of Chinese studies and the improvement of public understanding of China. In large measure, they grew out of the Ford Foundation's developmental program for "Research and Training on China," adopted in 1959. The staff proposal which the trustees of the Ford Foundation accepted at that time concluded that "the highest priority must be attached to the basic task of producing an expanded body of knowledge and a new group of competent specialists."

The task, as envisioned in the proposal, would "require major and continuing efforts over the decade ahead." It was not to be limited to the United States but to include countries in Europe and Asia with unique perspectives, opportunities, and resources that would be "of great value to American scholars in this field." Although the contributions of the National Defense Education Act were expected to make a strong contribution to this effort, "particularly in the language field," and modest support was anticipated from other sources of funds, the Ford Foundation accepted for itself a "major role."

As noted above—and apart from the official research undertaken within government agencies—the federal government, the Ford Foundation, and other governmental and private agencies have spent at least $40 million in support of academic training and research on China. The universities themselves, whose contributions were not assessed in this survey, have probably spent another $15 to $20 million to develop the field from general budgetary sources in the form of new teaching posts, support of research, library development, staff, student and administrative support, space and facilities. The total investment in this period for development from all these sources probably exceeds $70 million.

What has been the result of this decade of effort to develop a basis for understanding China? The tasks set forth in the Foundation's program in 1959 have been energetically pursued and in many areas markedly forwarded.

As its first objective, the Foundation encouraged the organization, which it subsequently supported, of a national committee "to help plan, organize, coordinate, advise, and stimulate activities on a national level." This committee, the Joint Committee on Contemporary China, has played a major role in helping to achieve many of the nine specific tasks listed in the Foundation's program. Between 1960–61 and 1970–71, it made 140 grants to 127 postdoctoral scholars, who report some 200 publications as a result of Committee support.* It has also stimulated disciplinary developments through committees dealing with society, politics, economics, law, and research materials that have sponsored or will sponsor 36 conferences and seminars drawing more than 700 participants from the United States and abroad; encouraged and supported the development of Chinese studies in several other countries through its allied international Liaison Committee on the Study of Contemporary China; and supported the development of research, materials, and training facilities in Asia and the United States, such as the Universities Service Centre in Hong Kong, the Center for Chinese Research Materials in Washington, and the Inter-University Program for Chinese Language Studies in Taiwan.

The second major objective of the Foundation was the development of training and research programs on contemporary China at universities. Primary attention was to be given to programs at four universities already strong in both Chinese and Russian studies; some support to stimulate training and research at other universities with significant resources; and elsewhere support for individual scholars. The number of universities that offer both Chinese-language courses and Ph.D. programs has grown

* An additional nineteen grants and one renewal were awarded for 1971–72 in March, 1971.

to thirty-one in 1970. The strength of the programs at these universities varies considerably.

Augmenting these broad aims, the Foundation proposal set forth nine specific important and interrelated objectives. Brief comments follow these items.

1. To attract able young scholars, particularly from the social sciences, into Chinese studies: As noted above, the number of graduates students has greatly increased since 1960.

2. To improve Chinese language training methods and facilities: The bulk of the funds for these purposes has come from NDEA grants, with approximately $1.3 million from the Carnegie Corporation for Chinese language programs in secondary schools. Several universities used Ford grants to develop language courses for the special needs of social scientists.

3. Stimulation of training and research at universities and support of individual scholars has been referred to above.

4. To improve the procurement, organization, and distribution of research materials relating to contemporary China and to develop various basic research tools, including bibliographic guides, collections of documents, handbooks, and a digest of current Chinese Communist materials: The problem of procuring research materials, traditional and modern, to fill gaps in existing libraries and to develop new libraries has been tackled with energy, yet some major difficulties remain. As noted in Chapter V, the Chinese Materials and Research Aids Service Center has made perhaps 600,000 copies of volumes dealing with traditional and Republican China available in the United States and Europe during the past seven years. The rapid and solid development of Chinese resources in Canberra, Australia, would have been almost impossible, for example,

without this service. For the more recent period, development has depended upon the use of the holdings of the Union Research Institute in Hong Kong, either directly by researchers at the Universities Service Centre or through microfilms. The willingness of the U.S. Government to make its Hong Kong translation series available to scholars, and its current journal and newspaper holdings available through the Library of Congress has been absolutely essential for the study of post-1949 developments on mainland China. The enterprise of librarians at five university centers of Chinese studies and at the Hoover Institution at Stanford in garnering virtually all published materials known to exist outside of China has been a critical factor for work on current developments in that country. Finally, the Foundation-funded Center for Chinese Research Materials in Washington has systematized the procurement, reproduction, and distribution of modern and contemporary materials needed by scholars. Various kinds of basic research tools are finally beginning to appear, each the product of years of patient effort, wide-ranging collaboration, and almost daunting difficulties. The largest enterprise of its kind is the Chinese Society Bibliography Project. Using more than 200 specialists, five years, and over $350,000, the project has opened to researchers massive quantities of documentation on Chinese society, past and present, in all major languages, computer prepared, and published in three volumes.

5. To support important research projects on China, especially those relevant to contemporary China, including—if feasible—systematic interviewing of refugees: Individual research, some of it related to larger projects, has been supported by the Joint Committee on Contemporary China of the ACLS-SSRC. The largest coordinated research project has been its Committee on the Economy of China. It will have produced thirteen volumes in the course

of eight years. In this and other studies, particularly those relating to politics, social change, law, and public services, interviews with refugees in Hong Kong have made important contributions to our understanding and to many doctoral dissertations and monographic studies.

6. To promote research conferences and publication of research in this field: These activities have been sponsored by the Joint Committee on Contemporary China, the Committee on the Economy of China, *The China Quarterly,* and in particular by the major university centers.

7. To establish a base for research and training in Hong Kong: The Universities Service Centre has been of particular importance in promoting interviews by both senior graduate students and university scholars. It also has served the vital function of providing a substitute training site for students who cannot get to mainland China, but need to acquire some concrete sense of the quality of life and day-to-day developments in China.

8. To take advantage of opportunities which may arise for scholars to visit Communist China or other Communist areas on its periphery: As of January, 1971, there have been no opportunities for American students and scholars to visit China for research purposes.

9. To develop and make use of available trained personnel and of research materials relevant to the study of contemporary China in various Asian and European countries such as Japan, England, France, and India, as well as Taiwan and Hong Kong. (See Appendix V for details.)

For unanticipated but understandable reasons, this effort on the whole has not matched the results in some other fields of area studies, as measured in trained specialists or new bodies of information. There has been an important but modest growth in our knowledge of China, but few major or distinguished studies and, in some disciplines, a limited or even shrinking body of information and grasp of Chinese realities. As for the training of specialists, the number of students committed to advanced professional training has gone up markedly and the number of universities with advanced graduate programs in Chinese studies had increased to twenty-three by 1969. But the time required for training students has been prolonged and the number of completed doctorates less than expected. In addition, the quality of training has suffered, particularly in the social sciences where access to data has been sharply curtailed and appropriate field work impossible.

It has taken more than a decade to build the base for solid and integrated programs of training, research, and public information on China in the United States. The constructive use of existing talent and resources, so laboriously developed in the past decade, and setting the pattern and priorities for future development are the problems that face us now.

In many other countries, interest in China has also produced new academic and research programs. Although it is misleading to compare countries without taking account of unique conditions and proportionate size and resources, some of these new programs probably rival or even exceed those of the United States. Australia, for example, has made notable progress despite the higher priority it gives to Southeast Asian, South Asian, and Japanese studies. Germany is now embarked on a broad development of its resources and talent for understanding China. Among China's Asian neighbors, except for Japan, political fears have almost totally precluded any effort to build a body of knowledge and specialists on contemporary China. In some areas, where local Chinese populations are important, the study of traditional China has also been inhibited by the host countries. In the Soviet Union, the modest but distinguished tradition of Sinological studies has barely survived. Only in the last four years has contemporary China become the focus of major scientific concern in the universities and the Academy of Sciences. During the past few years, in Japan and leading nations of the non-Asian world, the growing stress in programs of training and research has been on modern and contemporary China, primarily in the social sciences but sometimes, as is true of Czechoslovakia, in modern literature.

China's domestic woes have a direct bearing on the course of Chinese studies and the problems of understanding China. Except for primitive societies, the knowledge of outsiders about a given country, even one that stringently controls access by outsiders because of war or a garrison-state political system, is usually based on the work of native or local scholars, data collection, and interpretative analysis. In China, after 1959, the statistical system collapsed first. Later, with the Cultural Revolution, the universities ceased normal activities, and large sectors of the research system came to a halt.

As a consequence, for more than a decade the political, economic, and social experience of one-fifth to one-quarter of the world's population has been underdocumented and recorded poorly or not at all.

Recommendations

The discussion above summarizes what was done in the 1960's to implement the Foundation's policy decisions of 1959. The recommendations which follow summarize what I believe now needs to be done in the decade of the 1970's. These recommendations are designed to

1. Safeguard investments that have been made to develop scarce national resources for understanding China
2. Repair weaknesses and gaps

3. Encourage both broader and more intensive educational and research use of existing resources

4. Improve the quality of scholarship and research

5. Lay a stronger groundwork for programs with broad social and public-affairs goals

6. Foster international understanding and improved relations with China

None of these purposes can be achieved easily or quickly. They represent a *direction* in which to channel our energies, resources, and available funds.

Insofar as the United States is concerned, these recommendations assume significant continuing federal support of centers and fellowship programs developed under the National Defense Education Act of 1958 and related acts. If federal support for these purposes should terminate in the near future, then a rapid expansion of privately funded fellowship programs would be needed immediately and for three or four subsequent years to enable the best of the present generation of advanced graduate students to complete their training. The recommendations also assume that continued growth and reorientation of higher and secondary education will provide teaching posts for these young scholars. Should this assumption prove false, it may be necessary to preserve such rare talents for the future by partial funding of temporary teaching posts at forward-looking institutions of higher education.

Because the large goals embodied in the International Education Act, which now has been set aside, can only be reached by a national effort, these recommendations further assume that fuller understanding of China during the next decade depends on improvements in the quality rather than the quantity of training and research, and on improved use of available and rare resources.

Although they are obviously and inescapably interrelated, these recommendations are presented in a rough order of descending priority.

RECOMMENDATION I

In order to maintain and improve training and research and to conserve critical assets for future development at a time of diminishing private and governmental resources for international studies and a cutback in educational growth, the strongest programs and facilities at a few major universities must have continuing and special support.

The following combination of assets characterizes the four or five universities with the strongest programs. These universities have trained the largest number of undergraduate and graduate students over the past ten years; they have the largest number of faculty members and the widest distribution of disciplinary specialists; and each offers at least 75 courses dealing with China. Each maintains a major library of Chinese publications adequate for multidisciplinary training and research, is recognized as a major center for visiting scholars from both this country and abroad, offers supporting programs dealing with East Asia, the Soviet Union, and international affairs, and has or is developing one or more associated professional programs covering China in such fields as law, medicine, education, journalism, or urban affairs. Finally, each has established centers or organizational bodies to foster interdisciplinary training and research, and to manage and support research projects, collections, and facilities.

It is at these centers (Harvard, Columbia, Michigan, Washington, the University of California at Berkeley), with their interdisciplinary staffs and sizable student bodies, that improved training programs can be most effectively developed and research of higher quality can be best fostered.

RECOMMENDATION II

Because of their relatively rich resources, these major university centers, as well as a handful of other universities with special strength in one or two fields (Chicago, Yale, Stanford, and Princeton), should make their facilities available on a regular or rotating basis to faculty members at the growing number of institutions committed to including China in their academic programs, but possessing only modest resources if any in Chinese studies. In order to sustain the morale and intellectual vitality of scholars at such institutions, provision might be made for many of them to be linked to neighboring major institutions as research associates and as participants in regionally organized faculty seminars. Moreover, most senior graduate students doing their doctorates at smaller centers, usually under the direction of a single scholar, should have the opportunity to work for substantial periods at a major center.

RECOMMENDATION III

Because in the next decade the field will suffer from the attrition of seasoned scholars trained in China and the erosion of scholarship in China, it is important to improve radically the quality of training and scholarly equipment of the best of the current group of junior scholars and on-coming graduate students. This will require both a better command of the language as an active tool and a more intimate knowledge of Chinese society and tradition. By the end of the decade, there should be (apart from the language teachers) no fewer than 100 American scholars in a variety of fields who are effectively bilingual. To achieve this essential level of linguistic facility and cultural familiarity, additional time and funds for predoctoral or postdoctoral training will be required. In the long run, training programs should give a substantial number of American students part of their education in a Chinese-language institution where they compete with Chinese students.

RECOMMENDATION IV

In order to sustain research productivity and to reap the rewards of past educational commitment and investment, research grants should be continued and expanded to take into account the larger number of qualified applicants appearing each year. Sources of research funds, such as the National Science Foundation, should be more hospitable to social-science applicants concerned with China. Adequate awards are particularly needed for those whose research critically depends on field work.

RECOMMENDATION V

One or more special language-training facilities should be maintained in a Chinese culture area in Asia for advanced language training, but also with provision for students seeking to acquire mastery of the language through intensive study as undergraduates or at an early stage in their graduate work. With the expansion of university programs in many countries in Europe and Asia, where English is an acceptable medium of instruction, serious consideration should be given to developing international facilities for Chinese language training—on grounds of efficiency, spreading the cost, and the indirect benefits of intercultural associations. The Inter-University Program for Chinese Language Studies in Taipei is underutilized, and its present intensive, expensive, and segregated system of operations may not adequately serve to introduce students to the Chinese environment. The possibility of linking international research projects on linguistics with a language-teaching center likewise should be explored. In other words, it is essential that foreign and American students preparing for professional and advanced scholarly work on China be thoroughly immersed in a Chinese environment at least for a short period.

RECOMMENDATION VI

Because access to China for study and research will be restricted for the foreseeable future, even for those students and scholars able to visit China, the Universities Service Centre should be maintained in Hong Kong as an international training and research base for specialists on contemporary mainland Chinese affairs. There is a widespread view that its usefulness for graduate students could be substantially improved through formal and informal seminars supervised by a recognized scholar in residence. The quantity and quality of research on contemporary China in the United States and in several countries in Europe and Asia have been increased significantly by work done in Hong Kong, with a minimum amount of difficulty and restraint, by virtue of the Centre's facilities.

Under present conditions, there is no substitute for Hong Kong. The political prerequisites for international scholarly use of Hong Kong on an efficient and regular basis appears to be the existence of a facility or facilities to accommodate and legitimize the activities of students and scholars.

RECOMMENDATION VII

Despite the developmental efforts of the past decade, certain disciplines or areas remain weak or have been neglected. In the social sciences, a continuing effort should be made to triple the number of well-trained economists and to train a few outstanding individuals concerned with mainland China in certain other neglected fields—anthropology, demography, linguistics, social psychology, and sociology. Studies of Chinese science and technology, medicine and public health, urban and environmental policies and problems—all neglected thus far as coherent or significant fields of study—need to be inaugurated or expanded. The first step is support of a few collaborative projects of study in each of these fields that would bring together area and professional specialists. International cooperation would increase the possibility in some cases of uniting the experiences of professionally qualified visitors to mainland China and the work of specialists on China.

As a few talented students and researchers appear with highly specialized interests in the Chinese experience in these fields, they should be assisted in finding institutional associations where they can continue their work.

RECOMMENDATION VIII

Despite inadequacies, the United States now has in many fields scholars, training programs, facilities, and organizational and research resources for the study and understanding of China that are unmatched by other countries. At the same time, American understanding of China is dependent in critical respects on the materials, experience, and scholarship of specialists in other countries who have different perspectives and greater access to China. Global perspectives on China should challenge and replace parochial views. American cooperation with scholars and specialists in other countries can be achieved through research conferences, projects calling for collaborative research, exchange of teaching and research materials, scholarly exchanges, and, in special cases, American assistance to countries seeking to develop their own independent training programs and research facilities for understanding China. To avoid political complications, these efforts should be carefully planned. Bodies now engaged in such enterprises can be used to sustain and develop these projects and interchanges.

RECOMMENDATION IX

Adequate research materials and aids continue to present problems for those in Chinese studies. The Chinese Materials and Research Aids Service Center in Taipei will continue to perform a valuable international service for the foreseeable future. Its preparation of research aids dealing with traditional and Republican China should be improved. With respect to materials relating to contemporary China, the long-term need for the services of the Center for Chinese Research Materials in Washington, D.C., is unpredictable, depending on the availability of materials in China. The decision to maintain and possibly restructure this center will depend upon circumstances at the time new sources of support must be sought. Control of information may become more important than acquisition and distribution. However, in view of current uncertainties and the fact that the work of scholars in the field will suffer if adequate efforts are not made to provide them with research data, this center should be preserved for the present.

RECOMMENDATION X

Improved public understanding of China depends on a complex set of factors. In the long run, there is little doubt that the educational system in each country is the single most important vehicle for inculcating knowledge about China and providing wider and more objective perspectives on China. Access to education and the aims of the educational system differ from country to country. In the United States, with its decentralized educational system, the treatment China receives in various widely used textbook series and in other classroom materials, as in the case of black studies, is perhaps crucial.

The growing number of undergraduate majors on China in the United States and in several countries in Europe and Asia provides a pool from which to recruit textbook writers and others to undertake a variety of public-information activities. Recommendations for procedures to review textbooks and to prepare new materials for secondary schools should be sought from those in the field.

On a world-wide basis, a preliminary but fundamental measure for improving understanding of China among strategic audiences with diverse interests is the incorporation of information about China in the regular reports and study series issued by such international agencies as the World Health Organization, the Food and Agriculture Organization, the Economic Commission for Asia and the Far East, the International Congress of Scientific Unions, UNESCO, and the Organization for Economic Cooperation and Development, as well as various nongovernmental bodies. Such inclusion of China in the world scene would appear to be a basic first step in promoting official and public enlightenment. Therefore, insofar as political problems can be surmounted, a prompt effort should be made to explore measures necessary to change the reporting and publication policies of international bodies.

Although no single program or effort can be relied upon to increase world-wide understanding of China, the growing sophistication and reach of communications technology underline the importance of the mass media. The volume and character of the attention given to China depends upon many factors. One basic factor is employment by all the major information systems of specialists on China, qualified and committed to provide an objective portrayal of Chinese developments. As more undergraduate majors emerge, the opportunity to recruit and place individuals with suitable training improves. The point now has been reached where an appropriate organization or institution should be asked to develop procedures to augment the resources of the mass media, both in the United States and in other countries, for disseminating information about China, including information originating in China.

As more scholars are trained to take up posts around the country and as major centers become better staffed and the burdens of teaching and research are lightened, many faculty members might be induced to assist in the preparation of programs and materials for public rather than specialist use. The vocational functions of university centers and scholars can be more broadly conceived.

Finally, continuing efforts by many groups to communicate with mainland Chinese should be encouraged. The effort itself is educational, directly and indirectly. In addition, these exploratory processes can have wider influence if they are associated with studies or conferences that organize information about China in such relevant fields as business and industry, science and technology, education and culture, and medicine and public health.

Appendix I: Institutions in which Chinese is Taught

Antioch College
Arizona State University
Arizona, University of
Armstrong College of
  Savannah
Beloit College
Boston College
Brigham Young University
Brooklyn College (CUNY)
Brown University
Cabrillo College
California State College
  (Dominguez Hills)
California State College
  (Los Angeles)
California, University of
  (Berkeley)
California, University of
  (Davis)
California, University of
  (La Jolla)
California, University of
  (Los Angeles)
California, University of

(Santa Barbara)
Canisius College
Central Connecticut State
  College
Chicago, University of
Church College of Hawaii
Claremont College
Colorado, University of
Columbia University
Connecticut College
Cornell University
Dartmouth College
DePauw University
Duke University
Eastern Washington State
  College
Edinboro State College
  (Penn.)
Fairleigh Dickinson University
Florida Presbyterian College
Florida State University
Franklin & Marshall College
Georgetown University
George Washington University

Georgia Institute of
Technology
Harvard University
Hawaii, University of
(Honolulu)
Hofstra University
Hunter College (CUNY)
Illinois, University of
Indiana State University
Indiana, University of
Indiana University (Penn.)
Iowa State University
Iowa, University of
Kalamazoo College
Kansas, University of
Leeward Community College
(Hawaii)
Los Angeles City College
Manhattanville College
Maryland, University of
Massachusetts, University of
Merritt College
Miami University (Ohio)
Miami, University of
Michigan State University
Michigan, University of
Milligan College
Minnesota, University of
Monterey Institute of Foreign
Studies
Monterey Peninsula College
Morehouse College
New York State University
College (Brockport)
New York, State University
College of Home
Economics (Cornell)
New York State University

College (Geneseo)
New York State University
College (New Paltz)
New York State University
College (Oneonta)
New York State University
College (Plattsburgh)
New York, State University
of, Albany
New York, State University
of, Buffalo
New York, State University
of, New Paltz
New York, State University
of, Stony Brook
New York University
North Carolina, University of
(Chapel Hill)
North Park College and
Theological Seminary
Oakland University
Oberlin College
Ohio State University
Oregon, University of
Pasadena City College
Pennsylvania State University
Pennsylvania, University of
Pittsburgh, University of
Pitzer College
Pomona College
Princeton University
Queens College (CUNY)
Radcliffe College
Rochester, University of
Rockford College
Rutgers University
St. Benedict, College of
(Minn.)

St. Elizabeth, College of
(N.J.)
St. Mary of the Woods
College (Ind.)
San Diego State College
San Fernando Valley State
College
San Francisco, City College of
San Francisco State College
Scripps College
Seton Hall University
Smith College
South Dakota, University of
Southern California,
University of
Southern Illinois College
Southern Illinois University
Stanford University
Stanislaus State College
(Calif.)
Texas Technical College
Texas, University of (Austin)

Union College
U.S. Air Force Academy
U.S. Military Academy
U.S. Naval Academy
Utah, University of
Vanderbilt University
Vassar College
Virginia Commonwealth
University
Virginia, University of
Wabash College
Washington University (Mo.)
Washington, University of
Western Kentucky State
College
Wellesley College
Western Michigan College
Winthrop College
Wisconsin, University of
(Madison)
Wittenberg University
Yale University

* Compiled partially from "Table 18," *Foreign Language Registrations and Student Contact Hours in Institutions of Higher Education, Fall 1968 and Summer 1969,* issued by The Modern Language Association of America, November, 1969, pp. 47–48.

American Universities and Colleges with Undergraduate Enrollments in Chinese Language Courses, Fall, 1968 *

Institutions	Enroll-ments	Institutions	Enroll-ments
Antioch College	3	Brigham Young	
Arizona State University	53	University	89
Arizona, University of	38	Brooklyn College, City	
Beloit College	12	University of New York	60

Institutions	Enroll-ments	Institutions	Enroll-ments
Brown University	20	Georgetown University	29
Cabrillo College	12	George Washington	
California State College-Dominguez Hills	6	University	101
		Harvard University	?
California State College-Los Angeles	32	Hawaii, University of	170
		Hofstra University	13
California, University of, at Berkeley	138	Hunter College, City University of New York	37
California, University of, at Davis	48	Illinois, University of	59
		Indiana State University	27
California, University of, at La Jolla	2	Indiana, University of	108
		Indiana University, Pennsylvania	78
California, University of, at Los Angeles	156	Iowa State University	5
		Iowa, University of	168
California, University of, at Santa Barbara	60	Kalamazoo College	3
		Kansas, University of	54
Canisius College	3	Leeward Community College	3
Central Connecticut State College	24	Los Angeles City College	103
Chicago, University of	92	Manhattanville College	11
Colorado, University of	78	Maryland, University of	65
Columbia University	120	Merritt College	39
Connecticut College	34	Miami University, Ohio	31
Cornell University	43	Miami, University of	29
Dartmouth College	14	Michigan State University	38
Duke University	8	Michigan, University of	88
Eastern Washington State College	10	Milligan College	5
		Minnesota, University of	45
Edinboro State College	5	Monterey Institute of Foreign Studies	15
Fairleigh Dickinson University	15	Monterey Peninsula College	14
Florida Presbyterian College	23	Morehouse College	6
Franklin & Marshall College	4		

Institutions	Enroll-ments	Institutions	Enroll-ments
New York State University College, Brockport	2	Rutgers University	42
		St. Benedict, College of	11
		St. Elizabeth, College of	4
New York State University College, Geneseo	2	St. Mary of the Woods College	5
		San Diego State College	23
New York State University College, New Paltz	24	San Fernando Valley State College	18
		San Francisco, City College of	114
New York State University College, Oneonta	1	San Francisco State College	189
		Scripps College	1
New York State University College, Plattsburgh	4	Seton Hall University	22
		Smith College	19
New York, State University of, Albany	13	Southern California, University of	87
		Southern Illinois College	47
New York State University of, Buffalo	8	Stanford University	42
		Stanislaus State College	1
New York State University of, Stony Brook	25	Texas Technical College	9
		Texas, University of, Austin	46
New York University	29	Union College	19
North Park College	8	U.S. Air Force Academy	24
Oakland University	40	U.S. Military Academy	71
Oberlin College	28	U.S. Naval Academy	20
Ohio State University	133	Utah, University of	21
Oregon, University of	38	Vanderbilt University	8
Pasadena City College	9	Vassar College	41
Pennsylvania State University	25	Virginia Commonwealth University	11
Pittsburgh, University of	59	Virginia, University of	18
Princeton University	22	Wabash College	29
Rochester, University of	24	Washington, University of	40
Rockford College	10		

Institutions	Enroll-ments	Institutions	Enroll-ments
Washington University, Mo.	36	Wisconsin, University of, Madison	87
Wellesley College	24	Wittenberg University	14
Winthrop College	12	Yale University	25
Total number of enrollments			4,230
Total number of institutions			111

Data on 1968 Course Enrollments Not Available

Armstrong College of
  Savannah
Boston College
Church College of Hawaii
Claremont College
De Pauw University
Florida State University
Georgia Institute of
  Technology
Massachusetts, University of
North Carolina, University of

(Chapel Hill)
Pennsylvania, University of
Pitzer College
Pomona College
Queens College
Radcliffe College
South Dakota, University of
Southern Illinois University
Western Kentucky State
  College
Western Michigan College

* Compiled from "Foreign Language Registrations in Institutions of Higher Education, Fall, 1968," *Foreign Language Annals,* III, 2 (December, 1969), 282–97.

*American Universities with Graduate Enrollments in Chinese Language Courses, Fall, 1968 **

Universities	Enroll-ments	Institutions	Enroll-ments
Arizona, University of	10	California, University of, at Davis	
Brown University	11		
California, University of, at Berkeley	43	California University of, at La Jolla	1

Institutions	Enroll-ments	Institutions	Enroll-ments
California, University of, at Los Angeles	6	Pennsylvania State University	4
Chicago, University of	49	Pittsburgh, University of	2
Columbia University	111	San Francisco State College	28
Georgetown University	10	Seton Hall University	55
Harvard University	?	Smith College	1
Hawaii, University of	88	Southern California, University of	27
Indiana, University of	40	Southern Illinois University	4
Iowa, University of	6		
Miami, University of	2	Stanford University	42
Michigan State University	6	Washington University, Mo.	1
Michigan, University of	81	Washington, University of	58
Minnesota, University of	9	Wisconsin, University of	59
Monterey Institute of Foreign Studies	14	Yale University	20
North Carolina, University of	21		
Ohio State University	16		

Total number of enrollments	831
Total number of institutions	32

* Compiled from "Foreign Language Registrations in Institutions of Higher Education, Fall, 1968," *Foreign Language Annals,* III, 2 (December, 1969), 282–97.

Appendix II: Chinese Language Instruction in Secondary Schools

Between 150 and 200 American secondary schools have introduced Chinese language courses, some as early as the seventh grade and offering up to four years of instruction. Total enrollment during the past few years appears to be between 2,000 and 2,500. Because of their Chinese-American population, California and Hawaii clearly are in the lead and in 1968 had 813 and 420 students enrolled respectively.

It should be noted that while enrollments in first-year courses number over 1,000, the number drops sharply in subsequent years. This highlights a problem about Chinese as a second language: a disjuncture between the spoken and written forms of the language and the impossibility of learning both at the same rate. Even four years of non-intensive secondary school study probably gives students less usable command of the language in written form than two years of study of one of the modern European languages. This, however, does not mean that it should not be taught in secondary schools. It does suggest the desirability of closely relating Chinese language work to the study of Chinese culture and history. The study of the language can be particularly effective and perhaps essential as an instrument to introduce the student to unique features of Chinese civilization. Moreover, students from Chinese-speaking homes are a special case because their home settings may reinforce what they have learned at school.

Chinese is taught also in a few secondary schools on an experimental basis in England, France, Sweden, and the Soviet Union. Among the scholars with whom I discussed this matter

ENROLLMENTS IN CHINESE LANGUAGE IN SECONDARY SCHOOLS, BY STATE, WITH BREAKDOWN BY COURSES, FALL, 1968

Languages and States Where Taught	Course I Enrollment			Course II Enroll- ment	Course III Enroll- ment	Course IV Enroll- ment	Unclas- sified (No Breakdown by Level Available)	Total Enroll- ment in All Courses
	Total Grades 7–12	Grades 7–8	Grades 9–12					
1	*2*	*3*	*4*	*5*	*6*	*7*	*8*	*9*
CHINESE								
Arizona	67	0	67	14	0	1	0	82
California	586	250	336	169	43	15	0	813
D. of Columbia	2	0	2	6	0	0	0	8
Florida	26	0	26	0	0	0	0	26
Georgia	17	0	17	30	0	0	0	47
Hawaii	253	112	141	123	34	10	0	420
Illinois	0	0	0	4	0	2	1	7
Indiana	1	0	1	3	0	0	0	4
Minnesota	10	0	10	9	0	0	0	19
New Jersey	104	0	104	29	2	0	0	135
New York	0	0	0	0	0	0	267	267
Ohio	39	0	39	12	4	0	0	55
Pennsylvania	80	0	80	28	0	0	0	108
Utah	11	0	11	4	5	0	0	20
Washington	49	0	49	36	0	0	0	85
Totals	*1,245*	*362*	*883*	*467*	*88*	*28*	*268*	*2,096*

in these countries, few were enthusiastic about the results. In England and Russia, in particular, there were those who felt that intensive language study was necessary in learning Chinese at a pace which was rewarding for both students and teachers. They argued that the amount of course time and student incentives were lacking for such commitment to Chinese at the secondary level. A second complaint in these countries and also in this country has been the complete dependence in most schools on a single teacher for the program. The teaching force and reserves are so small at present as to make teacher recruitment and replacement a matter of chance and the continuity and quality of a Chinese language program a matter of accidental good fortune.

The goal of broadening and universalizing the educational system to encompass exposure to non-Western civilizations seems to require persistence in overcoming these obstacles. To cut language out of the infusion of knowledge and understanding of China because of its difficulty cripples the effort. Moreover, the desire of Americans of Chinese origin to keep alive the Chinese component in our national culture is as legitimate as the desire of other groups. Undoubtedly, many states with goups desiring such language study will be responsive to their wishes. (At present the number of students studying Chinese [2000 plus] and Japanese [4000 plus], for example, reflects the proportion of the two groups in the American population, about 300,000 and 600,000.) For others, it may be desirable to subordinate the study of the Chinese language to the study of the culture and civilization of China and more fully integrate language work with such courses, both as part of general surveys and in courses specialized on China as a cultural region. The NDEA Summer Institutes for teachers of Chinese have played a useful role in providing experience and materials for the development of both language and social studies in the Chinese field. With the expansion of Chinese as an undergraduate field of specialization, a growing corps of potential teachers in secondary schools becomes available. This will reduce some of the problems that have existed in the past and, indeed, provide a natural vocational use for the special training of undergraduates in the field.

APPENDIX III: DOCTORATES AWARDED IN CHINESE STUDIES
IN THE UNITED STATES, BY DISCIPLINE, 1960–69 *

Discipline	1960	1961	1962	1963	1964	1965	1966	1967	1968	1969	Total
History	9(2)	8(1)	15(6)	15(5)	9(2)	12(4)	13(3)	26(11)	20(3)	22(7)	149(44)
Political Science	1	1	6(4)	8(3)	1	8(4)	8(4)	9(4)	14(4)	19(5)	75(28)
Literature	1		3(2)	3	3(2)	6(2)	12(4)	5(3)	6(3)	10(4)	49(20)
Linguistics		1	1		3(2)	4(2)	12(4)	4(2)	5(3)	4(1)	34(14)
Anthropology	2(1)	2	1	1	4	1	3	5	4(2)	4(3)	27(6)
Economics	1(1)	1(1)	4(1)	1	3(2)	2(2)	4(3)		1	4(1)	21(11)
Art		1(1)	1(1)		2	2		2	2	1	11(2)
Geography		2(1)			2	1		3(1)	1	1	10(2)
Education & Psychology				1(1)	1(1)	1(1)	2(1)	1(1)			7(5)
Religion	2(1)	1(1)	1			1		1(1)	2(1)		8(4)
Law								2(1)	2		4(1)
Demography				1(1)						1	2(1)
Music	1(1)				1(1)				1		3(2)
Library Science									1	1(1)	2(1)
Philosophy					1		1(1)				2(1)

Discipline	1960	1961	1962	1963	1964	1965	1966	1967	1968	1969	Total
Sociology			1(1)				1	1		1	4(1)
Agricultural Economics							1(1)				1(1)
Archeology							1				1
Business Administration				1(1)							1(1)
History of Science						1					1
Totals:	17(6)	18(5)	33(15)	31(11)	30(10)	38(15)	59(21)	59(24)	59(16)	68(22)	412(145)

* Figures in parentheses indicate the number of students among degree recipients who are native speakers of Chinese.

APPENDIX IV: DOCTORATES AWARDED IN CHINESE STUDIES, BY INSTITUTION, 1960–69 *

Listed in Rank Order	1960	1961	1962	1963	1964	1965	1966	1967	1968	1969	Total
Harvard	3(1)	4	5(4)	9	5(2)	2	10(1)	8(3)	11	8(5)	65(16)
Columbia	1	1(1)	4	3	4(1)	3(1)	9(4)	8(4)	4	11(3)	48(14)
U. of California (Berkeley)	1	4	4(1)	1(1)	4(1)	6(1)		4	4(1)	7(2)	35(7)
Washington		2(1)	4(1)	1(1)	3	3(1)	7(3)	2(1)	5(1)	6	33(9)
Chicago	3	1	5(2)	1	2	1(1)		1	5	6(2)	25(5)
Indiana			1(1)	1(1)		1(1)	7(4)	1	2(1)	4(1)	18(10)
Pennsylvania	1		1(1)	1(1)			2	5(2)	4(2)	2(1)	16(7)
Michigan	1		1(1)	1	1	1(1)	2(1)	3	3(1)	3(2)	15(6)
Yale			2(2)		1	3	1	4(1)	2	2	15(3)
Georgetown	1(1)	1(1)		2	1(1)	2		2(1)	2(1)	3(2)	14(7)
New York University	1			4(3)		3(2)		1(1)	1(1)	1(1)	12(8)
Claremont					1	2	3	2(2)		1	9(2)
Cornell		1			1	1	2		2(2)	2(1)	9(3)
Wisconsin			1	3		1(1)		2(1)	2(1)	1(1)	7(4)

Listed in Rank Order	1960	1961	1962	1963	1964	1965	1966	1967	1968	1969	Total
Stanford	2(1)				2(1)	1(1)	1		1	1	8(3)
Princeton					1(1)	2	1(1)	3(1)	1	1	8(3)
UCLA			1			2(1)	1(1)	1(1)	1		6(3)
American U.							2(2)		2(1)	1	5(3)
Minnesota			2	1				1		1	5
USC					1(1)	1(1)		1(1)		1	4(3)
Illinois						1(1)			2(2)		3(3)
M.I.T.							2		1(1)		3(1)

* Figures in parentheses indicate the number of students among degree recipients who are native speakers of Chinese. These Ph.D.'s used Chinese source materials in their dissertations.

APPENDIX IV: DOCTORATES AWARDED IN CHINESE STUDIES,
BY INSTITUTION, 1960–69 *
(Continued)

Listed in Rank Order	1960	1961	1962	1963	1964	1965	1966	1967	1968	1969	Total
Pittsburgh								1	1	1	3
Texas	1(1)						2				3(1)
Colorado		1								1	2
Fordham			1(1)				1(1)				2(2)
Kansas				1(1)				1			2(1)
Maryland						1(1)		1			2(1)
Michigan State					1		1(1)				2(1)
New School for Soc. Research					1(1)	1(1)					2(2)
Ohio State			1(1)				2				3(1)
Radcliffe	2 (2)										2(2)
Southern Illinois				1(1)			1(1)				2(2)
Syracuse		1								1	2
Alabama										1(1)	1(1)
Bryn Mawr		1(1)									1(1)
Catholic									1		1

Listed in Rank Order	1960	1961	1962	1963	1964	1965	1966	1967	1968	1969	Total
Denver								1			1
Iowa								1			1
Iowa State							1(1)				1(1)
Louisiana								1(1)			1(1)
Massachusetts								1(1)			1(1)
Missouri								1(1)			1(1)
North Carolina				1							1

Listed in Rank Order	1960	1961	1962	1963	1964	1965	1966	1967	1968	1969	Total
Northwestern				1(1)							1(1)
Oregon								1(1)			1(1)
Pacific School of Religion		1(1)									1(1)
Princeton Theological Sem.								1(1)			1(1)
Rochester										1	1
St. John's									1		1
SUNY (Buffalo)					1(1)						1(1)
Temple									1(1)		1(1)
Tufts							1				1
Union Theological Seminary											1
Virginia										1	1
George Washington										1	1
		1(1)	1	1(1)	1(1)		1	2(2)	2(1)	3	12(6)
Totals:	17(6)	18(5)	33(15)	33(11)	30(10)	38(15)	59(21)	59(24)	59(16)	68(22)	412(145)

(412 doctorates in ten years, of which 35% of recipients were native speakers of Chinese [145] and 65% were not [267].)

Appendix V: Ford Foundation Grants in Support of Chinese Studies

(Where grant is only partially for China an estimate [noted by "Est."] is made of the China portion)

I. *The Initial Period, 1952–58*

American Friends Service Committee
    1952: Seminars in the Far East   (Est.)   10,000
University of Washington
    1954: History of the Chinese
           Communist Party to 1938   12,200
    1956: Continuation of History of the
           Chinese Communist Party   28,260
    1956–57: Grants-in-aid to students   5,800
    1957: Research on Northeast Asia and
           International Relations-
           350,000   (Est.)   100,000

                                        $156,260

Stanford University
    1953: Hoover Institute and
           Library (225,000)   (Est.)   75,000
    1955: Program on China   15,000
    1956: Processing Materials on
           China and Japan   (Est.)   40,000

1955–57: Grants-in-aid to graduate students in Chinese studies		7,800
1958: Asian studies ($250,000)	(Est.)	140,500
		278,300

University of Chicago

1955: Program on China	22,500
1955–57: Grants-in-aid to students	7,800
	$30,300

Columbia University

1955: Research on Political Evolution of Modern China: Project on Men and Politics in Modern China		420,000
1956–58: Grants-in-aid to students	(Est.)	15,000
		$435,000

Harvard University

1955: Research and Publication on the Modern Chinese Economy		277,000
1956–57: Grants-in-aid to students	(Est.)	15,000
1958: International Studies: For Training and Research on the Modern Economy of China		300,000
		$592,000

Cornell University

1956: Inter-University Field Training in Chinese Language		153,600
1958: International Studies: For Field Training in Chinese Language—579,000	(Est.)	160,000
		$313,600

Modern Language Association of America
  1957: Analysis and Evaluation of
        Chinese Language Teaching   45,000

University of California (Berkeley)
  1955–57: Grants-in-aid to students   (Est.)   17,500
  1957: Advanced Training and Research
      on Modern China and Other
      Foreign Areas   350,000

                        $367,500

Georgetown University
  1958: Collection and Annotation of
      South Manchurian Railway
      Materials on China   25,000

American Council of Learned Societies
  1953: Survey of Asian and African
      Personnel Resources   (Est.)   1,000
  1956: Program for Compiling
      Dictionaries, Readers and
      Texts for Oriental Studies
      —250,000   (Est.)   100,000

                        $101,000

Association for Asian Studies
  1954, 1955: Support for *Far Eastern
      Quarterly* and Far Eastern
      Monograph Series—31,500   (Est.)   15,000
  1955: Training and Research on
      Asia—38,500   (Est.)   10,000

                        $25,000

Foreign Area Fellowship Program
(1952–58)   672,549

Miscellaneous 1952–58 (Est.) 85,000

Total $3,126,509

II. *The Developmental Decade, 1959–69*

1959

Columbia University
Grants-in-aid to graduate students
(9,610 for Asian Studies) (Est.) 5,000

Cornell University
Grants-in-aid to graduate students
(1,700 for Far Eastern Studies) (Est.) 1,000

Harvard University
Grants-in-aid to graduate students
(7,650 for Far Eastern Studies) (Est.) 5,000

University of Washington
Grants-in-aid to graduate students
(6,260 for Far Eastern Studies) (Est.) 4,000

Association for Asian Studies
Committee on American Library
Resources of the Far East
(China and Japan—6,400) (Est.) 4,000

$19,000

1960

Columbia University
Grants-in-aid to graduate students
(9,200 for Asian Studies) (Est.) 5,000

Cornell University
Grants-in-aid to graduate students
(1,500 for Far Eastern Studies) (Est.) 800

Harvard University
  Grants-in-aid to graduate students
  (8,000 for Far Eastern Studies)   (Est.)   4,000

University of Washington
  Grants-in-aid to graduate students
  (7,600 for Far Eastern Studies)   (Est.)   5,000

Social Science Research Council
  Grants-in-aid for research and
  related activities:
  Joint Committee on Contemporary
  China   250,000

Harvard University
  International Studies
  (5,600,000 for Center for East
  Asian Studies)   900,000

Columbia University
  East Asian Institute: Study of
  Contemporary China (5,500,000
  for International Studies)   795,000

University of California, Berkeley
  (4,000,000 for International Studies;
  1,300,000 for China and Japan
  Studies)   (Est.)   900,000

Spelman College
  (Non-Western Studies, 200,000)   (Est.)   50,000

Modern Language Association of America
  Analysis and Evaluation of
  Chinese Language Teaching   6,000
                                         _____
                                              $2,915,800

1961

Foreign Service Institute
Field Survey of Language Training
Facilities on Taiwan   2,500

Association for Asian Studies
Committee on Chinese Thought
(general support 165,000)   (Est.)   10,000

Columbia University
Grants-in-aid to graduate students
(7,000 for Asian Studies)   (Est.)   4,000

Cornell University
Grants-in-aid to graduate students
(1,500 for Far Eastern Studies)   (Est.)   800

Harvard University
Grants-in-aid to graduate students
(7,000 for Far Eastern Studies)   (Est.)   4,000

University of Washington
Grants-in-aid to graduate students
(5,000 for Far Eastern Studies)   (Est.)   3,000

Notre Dame
(265,000 for Program in Soviet
and East European Studies)   (Est.)   10,000

University of Chicago
(5,400,000 for International
Studies)   (Est.)   400,000

American Council of Learned Societies
(800,000 for Grants-in-aid on Asia,
Russia and Eastern Europe)   (Est.)   100,000

Indiana University
  (880,000 for International Studies,
  Asian and Near Eastern Program)   (Est.)   300,000

University of San Francisco
  Work on the Chinese Economy   10,818

University of Michigan
  China Program
  (3,000,000 for International Studies)   1,550,000

Princeton University
  (2,500,000 for International Studies;
  500,000 for China and Japan)   (Est.)   250,000

University of Washington
  China Studies
  (2,000,000 for International Studies)   1,400,000

Yale University
  Non-Western and International Studies
  (3,000,000)   300,000
                                           _____
                                          $4,345,118
                                           _____

1962

Social Science Research Council
  Exchanges with the Institute of
  Modern History, Academia Sinica,
  Taipei (165,000 for Committee on
  Exchanges with Asian Institutions)   80,000
  Research on the Chinese Economy   910,000
  Joint Committee on Contemporary
  China   420,000

Council on Foreign Relations
  Studies Relating to China and
  Policies toward China   450,000

Gettysburg College
(180,000 for China and India
Studies) (Est.) 90,000

Cornell University
China Program
(3,250,000 for International
Programs) 800,000

University of Wisconsin
(International Studies, 400,000 for
African and Far Eastern Studies) (Est.) 150,000

Miscellaneous 260,000

$3,160,000

1963

George Washington University
(145,000 for Program on Communist
China and Sino-Soviet Relations) (Est.) 100,000

American University
(151,000 for Program on Communist
China and Sino-Soviet Relations) (Est.) 100,000

Purdue Research Foundation
(256,000 for Study of Chinese and
Japanese by Beginner and
Intermediate Students) (Est.) 150,000

Stanford University
(338,000 for Inter-University
Language Centers in Chinese and
Japanese) (Est.) 150,000

Association for Asian Studies
Ming Biographical History Project 120,000

Washington University, St. Louis
(500,000 for International Studies) (Est.) 64,000

Columbia University
(160,000 for Cooperative Research
on the Law of Communist Societies) (Est.) 30,000

Stanford University
Strengthening of international studies
(2,500,000 for international studies;
900,000 for East Asian studies) (Est.) 550,000

$1,264,000

1964

Stanford University
(300,000 for Inter-University
Language Centers in Chinese and
Japanese) (Est.) 150,000

University of Illinois
(800,000 for International Studies;
250,000 for Asian Language and
Area Center) (Est.) 60,000

University of Hawaii
(300,000 for Pacific and Asian
Studies) (Est.) 100,000

University Center in Virginia
(130,000 for Summer Faculty
Seminars on Asia) (Est.) 50,000

University of Michigan
(110,000 for Faculty Seminars
on Asian Studies) (Est.) 25,000

$385,000

1965

Social Science Research Council
Joint Committee on Contemporary
China   900,000
Liaison Committee on Study of
Contemporary China   100,000

Gettysburg College
(40,000 for China and India Studies
Program)   (Est.)   20,000

Harvard University
China Law Program (12,500,000 for
International Studies)   (Est.)   500,000

Occidental College
(114,000 for Non-Western Studies) (Est.)   50,000

State College of Iowa
(156,000 for Inter-Cultural
Studies)   (Est.)   50,000

University of Washington
(600,000 for State-Wide Program in
Foreign Language Teaching;
188,000 for High School Program) (Est.)   30,000

                                   $1,650,000

1966

George Washington University
Institute for Sino-Soviet
Studies   (Est.)   200,000

Stanford University
Inter-University Chinese
Language Center, Taipei   318,000

Nelson Gallery Foundation		12,238
Princeton University Chinese Linguistics Project		330,000
Association for Asian Studies Chinese Materials and Research Aids Service Center (180,000 for general support)	(Est.)	25,000
American Council of Learned Societies (400,000 for research grants) China		200,000
University of Michigan (4,000,000 for International Studies Programs)	(Est.)	50,000
University of Washington (600,000 for Asian Law Program)	(Est.)	300,000
United Nations Association of the USA Panel on "China, the UN and US Policy"	(Est.)	100,000
		$1,535,238

1967

Harvard University East Asian Research Center	1,500,000
University of California, Berkeley Center for Chinese Studies	900,000
University of Michigan Center for Chinese Studies	900,000

Association of Research Libraries
  Center for Chinese Research
  Materials   500,000

Columbia University
  East Asian Institute   1,200,000

Cornell University
  China Studies Program   500,000

Purdue Research Foundation
  Summer Institutes in Chinese and
  Japanese Language (230,000 for
  Committee on Institutional
  Cooperation)   (Est.)   120,000

National Committee on U.S.-
China Relations   250,000

Smithsonian Institution
  Freer Gallery,
  Publications Fund   12,500

Social Science Research Council
  Committee on Exchanges with Asian
  Institutions; grants for research
  at the Academia Sinica, Taipei   85,000

Stanford University
  (6,000,000 for strengthening of
  international studies)   (Est.)   485,000
                                  $6,452,500

1968
Association for Asian Studies
  Ming Biographical History Project   120,000

American Council of Learned Societies
Joint Committee on Sino-American

Cooperation		150,000
Committee on Chinese Civilization		155,000
Committee on Asian Studies (242,000 for faculty research)	(Est.)	36,800

Education and World Affairs
Universities Service Centre,

Hong Kong		130,000
		$591,800

1969

National Committee on U.S.- China Relations		250,000
Yale University (150,000 for research seminar program in East Asian studies)	(Est.)	75,000
		$325,000

1959–70

Foreign Area Fellowship Program (130 grantees)		1,177,745
Total		$23,821,201

III. *Ford Foundation Support for Chinese Studies and Projects Outside the United States, 1958–70*

United Kingdom

1958: University of London	(Est.)	30,000
1959: Oxford University	(Est.)	100,000
1961: University of London	(Est.)	10,000
1963: Institute of Strategic Studies, London	(Est.)	5,000

1967:	University of London Contemporary China Institute		325,000
1967:	University of London	(Est.)	100,000
1967:	University of Leeds Library		50,000
1967:	London School of Economics and Political Science	(Est.)	100,000
1969:	Central Asian Research Center	(Est.)	20,000
			$740,000

Japan

1962:	Toyo Bunko		173,000
1963:	Kyoto University	(Est.)	50,000
1967:	Kyoto University	(Est.)	30,000
			$253,000

Republic of China: Taiwan

1962:	Academia Sinica		153,000
1967:	Academia Sinica		268,000
			$421,000

Australia

1963:	Australian National University	(Est.)	75,000
1967:	Australian National University	(Est.)	40,000
1968:	Australian Institute of International Affairs	(Est.)	10,000
			$125,000

Hong Kong

   1961: University of Hong Kong
           Conference on Economic and
           Social Problems of the Far
           East   (Est.)   10,000

India

   1964: University of Delhi   536,000

Korea

   1962: Asiatic Research Center   (Est.)   75,000
   1966: Asiatic Research Center   (Est.)   18,000
   1968: Asiatic Research Center   (Est.)   50,000

                                       $143,000

Germany

   1968: German Association for East
           Asian Studies   145,000
   1968: Institute for Asian Studies
           Hamburg   56,250
   1968: Free University of Berlin   40,000
   1968: University of Bochum   37,500
   1968: University of Munich   46,250

                                       $325,000

Canada

   1964: Humanities Research Council
           of Canada   (Est.)   17,000
   1968: Canadian Institute of
           International Affairs   80,000

                                        $97,000

International Association
    1967: Congress for Cultural Freedom:
          China Seminars and support
          for *The China Quarterly*   150,000
                          Total $2,800,000

Grand Total, Ford Foundation Grants
in Support of Chinese Studies
1952–70 $29,747,710

Index

(Individual universities are not listed in the Index.)

157